Life on Two Legs

Set The Record Straight

© Copyright MMXXIII Norman J Sheffield
All Rights Reserved.

Published by Trident Publishing Ltd
145-157 St Johns Street, London EC1V 4PY

First Printed, 2013
ISBN 978-0-9575133-1-0

A catalogue record for this book is available from the British Library

facebook.com/lifeontwolegs
twitter.com/lifeontwolegs
lifeontwolegs.com

Special thanks to Garry Jenkins
Designed by TridentPublishing.co.uk

Part of the proceeds from this book goes to support

Registered Charirty No. 1000025
www. matd.org.uk

Life on Two Legs

Set The Record Straight

Norman J Sheffield

TRIDENT
Trident Publishing

Acknowledgements

Special thanks to Chris for her encouragement and extreme patience and assistance with these stories, our children Darren, Russell Justin and Samantha for their constant love and support throughout the project and for finally convincing me to share the stories before they are forgotten forever!

Thanks to Garry Jenkins, Tony Bramwell, Nigel Grundy and Mick Rock for their contributions and support on this the project.

My thanks also go out to all those who helped me achieve my dream of opening Trident and my businesses since, and a special mention to Robert Iggulden, Peter Turner, Ken Osbourne, Gerry Salisbury, Dave Sampson and Patricia Johnston and Nick Wright.

This book is dedicated to my Grandchildren; Sebastian, Victoria, Mollie, Felix, Grace, Harrison, Amélie and also Arthur and Alexandra.

Interactivity

Why not listen along to the songs that form
part of the story while you read?

Mobile/Tablet QR Code for the Trident Studios Spotify® Playlist:

Alternatively use the following short URLs in any browser:
Spofity® Playlist URL: www.goo.gl/HU7M4 (Mobile or Desktop)
iTunes® Playlist Link: www.goo.gl/ChKab (Desktop Only)

Join the conversation:
facebook.com/lifeontwolegs
twitter.com/lifeontwolegs

Interactive full colour versions of this book
Available on the Apple iBooks®, Amazon Kindle®
and other popular eBook stores.

Contents

	Foreword, by Paul McCartney	9
Prologue	"Make It Better"	11
One	In And Out Of The Shadows	23
Two	Into The Alley	41
Three	Lord Of The Ringlets	63
Four	Sitting In A Tin Can	79
Five	New Horizons	105
Six	Meet The Queenies	117
Seven	Creative Differences	127
Eight	Doing Alright	141
Nine	Hitting The Road	165
Ten	Mr Big	179
Eleven	Freddiepoos	191
Twelve	I Want It All, And I Want It Now	215
Thirteen	Death On Two Legs	235
Fourteen	Out Of The Blue	249
Fifteen	Full Circle	269
Discography		278
The Team That Created it All		286

Foreword

by Paul McCartney

"Most of my early recording career with The Beatles took place in EMI's Abbey Road Studios but there were occasions when, for one reason or another, we worked in studios other than Abbey Road; Trident Studios was one of these. Its location in London's Soho was handy and slightly exotic. I remember enjoying many happy hours there including working on the Beatles 'Hey Jude'. The song had quite a long introduction before the drums came in and I seem to remember me starting and Ringo having to run to the toilet. He made it back just in time for his opening drum part and I have a feeling that that might well have been the take that we eventually used.

I knew Words cannot describe the pleasure of listening back to the final mix of 'Hey Jude' on four giant tanoy speakers which dwarfed everything else in the room. I was also there for many hours producing music by Mary Hopkins including her biggest hit 'Those Were the Days'. Much of James Taylor's first album was recorded there and even though I wasn't producing it I recollect dropping in and being asked by James to play bass on his song 'Carolina in My Mind'.

The people working there were always friendly and efficient and, besides making some cool music, we had plenty of good laughs. Fond memories of great days, in a great studio."

Prologue

"Make It Better"

"Nobody touch anything," George Martin said, clearly delighted with what he'd heard.

I was sitting in my office upstairs at the studio when the phone went. I recognised the voice on the other end of the line immediately; it was Peter Asher, the head of A&R at Apple Records in London.

"Norman, all hell's broken loose over at Abbey Road. So the boys are going to come over to you for a few days" he said. "Okay" I replied, sitting bolt upright in my chair and stubbing out a cigarette.

"We'll be there tomorrow afternoon. Keep it under your hat will you?," he said. "Don't want screaming hordes outside."

"Of course," I said "We'll make sure everything's ready. Anything I need to know?"

"They're doing this song Paul's written, 'Hey Jude'. If everything is okay they will be bringing in a thirty-six-piece orchestra."

It was only when I put the phone down that the significance of the call hit me.

"Bloody hell, this is it. The Beatles are coming!" I said to myself, running out of my office and heading downstairs to spread the news.

It was July 30th, 1968. Trident Studios, the recording facility I'd opened in Soho with my brother Barry five months earlier was still in its infancy. We were doing pretty well and slowly making our mark, attracting an eclectic range of artists from Manfred Mann and The Small Faces, to Apple acts like Mary Hopkin and an American newcomer named James Taylor, who Peter Asher had sent over to us. In particular, artists and producers were keen to try out our 8-track recording facilities, the first in the country, which we'd imported over from America.

But we'd experienced nothing to compare with the biggest band—and the four most famous people—on the entire planet.

This was something else entirely then.

In some ways it shouldn't have come as a total surprise that The Beatles were coming over to us. We had a good relationship with Apple Records, the Beatles' own record company, and they had booked some studio space a couple of days earlier. We'd recorded a lot of their acts before, so we'd assumed it was going to be used by one of them, perhaps Badfinger, who they were pushing at the time. Paul himself had been to Trident, producing Mary Hopkin and playing bass on James Taylor's record. Also I knew from Peter Asher that The Beatles and their producer George Martin had been having a hard time at Abbey Road, which had been long regarded as their "home" studio.

A film crew had been at work there at the same time. They had promised that the boys "wouldn't even know they were there," but it had been quite the opposite. The Beatles were perfectionists and the crew had been getting in the boys' way and making life difficult. Tensions had been running high. One of the EMI staff engineers at the time, Ken Scott, even reported that some fighting had been going on. The Beatles had said "enough", and now they'd decided to come to us.

It was the perfect opportunity; one that I'd secretly hoped would come up at some point. I'd opened the studio thinking it could be something very different to the antiseptic, almost laboratory atmosphere of Abbey Road and the other big studios. People there wore white coats and behaved like boffins. It sucked the creative life out of artists. From the outset I'd wanted Trident to be a place where musicians could be free to express themselves. I wanted a different vibe.

This would tell me whether we'd got it right. If The Beatles liked the studio then we'd really cracked it.

All these thoughts were running through my head as I whizzed through the four floors of the studio briefing the people who needed to know what was going to happen.

I spoke to my brother Barry, who would be engineering the recording with George Martin producing. I told him about the orchestra and he started making arrangements. I then headed downstairs to tell Chris, my wife, who was in reception working on bookings and admin.

Our studio was tucked away in the alleyway of St. Anne's Court, between Wardour Street and Dean Street in the heart of London's Soho district. If The Beatles' fanatical fans found out they were here, pandemonium would break out. And we didn't want that. So we dropped all the blinds down at the front of the building so people couldn't see into the reception room. The last thing we wanted was for Paul McCartney to be spotted in the front office then have a gang of girls screaming at him.

I knew the way The Beatles worked. They would want to get a bit of privacy. They were there to work, not to be hero-worshipped. Chris and I headed home that night feeling a mixture of anxiety and excitement. This really was it—the moment that would make us. Or maybe, if it went wrong, break us.

~

The next morning, as Peter Asher had promised, The Beatles' personal manager Mal Evans arrived with a truck. I went out to meet him and went round the back and saw that the truck was full of pot plants and tea chests.

"What are you doing?" I asked.

"We're here to make ourselves comfortable," Mal said, lugging a great big tea chest off the back of the truck.

I looked inside the chest. It was full of Corn Flakes and steaks in a packet.

"What the hell are you doing with all that food?" I asked.

"We had all this aggro with EMI's kitchen so we've got all this stuff for the boys to make sure it's okay."

"Leave it out Mal," I said. "We've got a full kitchen upstairs. If it's something peculiar they want, this is bloody Soho so we can get it."

He nodded and started putting the chest back inside the truck.

He insisted on the pot plants though.

Mal told me it was part of the hippy thing, which George and John in particular were into. The boys wanted them to make the place seem "soft." By now they'd started unloading the gear, including Ringo's drum kit. I recognised it, of course, as it was the same as the drum kit I had: a grey, pearl Ludwig set.

"He can use mine if he wants," I told Mel, dead serious.

He shook his head and carried on unloading it.

The boys started arriving just after lunchtime. The studio was booked from 2 p.m. that afternoon. Paul was one of the first to pitch up, then John, who had just broken up with his wife Cynthia and had just started going out with a Japanese artist called Yoko Ono. I'd half expected her to turn up. I'd heard there were tensions within the band about the way she stuck like glue to John, even going to the toilet with him apparently.

There was nothing starry about the boys. They were dressed for work: John in a white t-shirt and waistcoat, Paul in a scruffy grey wool jumper, and George—the best dressed of them—in a floral shirt and pinstripe trousers. I can't remember what Ringo wore.

That first day they worked solidly for fourteen hours, from two in the afternoon until four in the morning. Paul seemed to be leading things. The song started with him playing our hundred-year-old Bechstein piano and singing a vocal over the top while the other three backed him. I discovered that Paul had originally called the song "Hey Jules" and that it had been dedicated to John's son, Julian. Paul was really close to Cynthia Lennon and had been round to see her after John had left.

There were rumours that John wasn't happy about the song, but I saw no evidence of that. I left them to it in the studio. By the time they finally finished in the small hours of the morning they had got the basic rhythm track down in four takes.

It was a long and pretty intense session. But it wasn't all serious business—there were laughs too.

At one point they started another take of the song, with Paul playing the piano. It was a long lead in to the moment when the rest of the band came in, and halfway through everyone noticed that

Ringo wasn't there. It turned out he'd gone to the toilet.

Paul was just getting to the point where the drums came in when Ringo appeared in the corner of the studio and started tiptoeing towards his kit. He crept past Paul's back and arrived on his stool almost at the exact beat when he needed to come in. He couldn't have timed it better. Everyone collapsed with laughter in the control room upstairs.

Later in the session, when I wasn't there, one of the boys was caught swearing on tape. There were two versions of the story. According to one, Paul got the fingering wrong on his piano music. Everyone knew it because he said, "hit the wrong chord" followed by "oh fucking hell."

One of our engineers, Malcolm Toft, who did some mixing on the track, claimed that it was Lennon. According to him, Barry—who was doing the engineering—had sent a massive "foldback" level into John's headphones which had made him go "whoa" and then "fucking hell." It hadn't been possible to remove it, so John Lennon, always the joker of the band, insisted that it was left on the recording, "buried low enough" so that most people wouldn't be able to spot it. "But we'll know it's there," he'd said.

~

Despite all this, everyone headed home in the small hours happy with the way the first session had gone. But we knew that the following day would be the most testing one. Apparently they'd booked the orchestra at extremely short notice, so there would be a real mix of youth and experience. We were soon welcoming all sorts of characters carrying violin, bassoon, and cello cases.

Unfortunately, they weren't the only new arrivals. By lunchtime on the second day there was a crowd of fans hanging around Wardour Street and the entrance to St. Anne's Court. They were watching every entrance and exit, ready to pounce if they saw one of the "Fab Four" emerge into the daylight. We'd been rumbled.

It turned out we would have got away with our secret for a day or so, maybe even until they'd finished recording. But some idiot doorman at Abbey Road blew our cover and told the fans perpetually gathered outside.

He'd seen them gathering as usual that morning and gone up to them:

"There's no point you being here. You should be at Trident," he'd said.

A member of staff, Gerry Salisbury, who was acting as our security guy, had his hands full keeping the fans at bay and had to enlist a couple of helpers to maintain order. We just about managed to make sure they didn't disturb what was going on inside.

By the evening the entire orchestra had gathered inside the studio. A couple of them were well known in the rock industry. Bobby Kok was a cellist, and Bill Jackman, who was playing flute in this session, had played saxophone for The Beatles on "Lady Madonna". The rest were a mix of session musicians and classical musicians who'd been rounded up at short notice.

George Martin had written the orchestral arrangement, which was to come in during the final part of the seven-minute song.

There was a lot of dissent to start with. Some of the musicians were looking down their noses at The Beatles a bit, I think.

Paul picked up on this and confronted them straight away. "Do you guys want to get fucking paid or not?" he said.

That concentrated their minds pretty well. They were being paid a normal session fee of £25 which was very good for classical musicians. They soon fell into line.

I'd heard that Paul really drove the band on during the recording process, and it was obvious that it was true.

At one point Paul wanted them to sing the "la la la's" along as well, and agreed to pay them a "double fee" for it. Most of them had no problem at all, but one did. He walked out and said, "I'm not going to sing along and play bloody Paul McCartney's song."

It was his loss.

During the first takes, Paul wasn't happy with the energy and enthusiasm they were putting into it. So at one point he stood up on the grand piano and started conducting the orchestra, trying to work them up a bit.

As the night wore on, I was becoming more and more relaxed about it all. Things were going pretty well and Barry had told me that the recording was sounding good already. I headed up to my office to sort through some stuff and have a drink with Chris O'Dell and some of the people from Apple.

~

The boys were back again the next day to put the finishing touches to what they'd laid down during the first two days. They did some more overdubbing from 2 p.m. until just before midnight. We then did the stereo mixing until 1.30 a.m. By the time we'd finished it was Saturday morning, but no one was heading anywhere. Barry had produced an amazing stereo mix, and everyone was over the moon.

I knew the equipment we'd installed was the best in both London and the UK by a mile. In particular, we'd installed some Lockwood speakers which really were exceptional. But even I was impressed by the sound that came out.

I can still see the expressions in the cramped control room. Everyone's faces just froze. It was this amazing, massive, stereo sound, something that even The Beatles hadn't heard before. Everybody in the room was just blown away. The reaction from George and the boys was instant.

"Nobody touch anything,!" George Martin said, clearly delighted with what he'd heard.

"Can you play it again louder?" John said, drawing looks from everyone else.

"You can't play it any louder. It will blow your ears off!!" Barry said, to which he and everyone else laughed.

I could tell they were all really pleased. Paul grabbed the phone in the studio and rang over to the Apple offices where he asked for Peter Asher.

"Peter, come round here and have a listen to this," he said. At that moment, I knew we'd cracked it.

The Beatles released "Hey Jude" at the end of August in both the US and the UK, and it went straight to the top of the charts. (Ironically it was knocked off the top here in Britain by another record we recorded for Apple, Mary Hopkin's "Those Were the Days".) We had a few arguments with EMI over at Abbey Road about the mono mix. They claimed they couldn't use the 8-track stereo mix we'd done. They'd just bought some 8-track equipment but hadn't integrated it yet into their studio. The truth was it was sour grapes. They didn't know what to do with our tracks and besides; I didn't really care what they thought. I knew George Martin and The Beatles were happy and so was I, because I knew what it meant for us.

EMI paid us at our standard rate of £25 an hour. Those three or four days earned us as a studio around £1,000, but that wasn't the point. The value of those four days was priceless and beyond words. To have had The Beatles in there—and for them to have left raving about the place the way they did—was the break I'd been praying for.

When I first opened the studio we knew we were taking a huge gamble. But at the end of those four days, the gamble looked like it was going to pay off. And it did.

In the aftermath of the "Hey Jude" recording, Trident Studios welcomed some of the greatest talents of the sixties and seventies, from Elton John to David Bowie, Marc Bolan to Frank Zappa. We went on to record some of the most famous albums of all time, from Hunky Dory and Goodbye Yellow Brick Road, to Sheer Heart Attack and the The White Album: We didn't stop there. We also launched one of the first broadcast video companies, a cassette manufacturing company, and the famous Trident Recording consoles. Last but not least, we launched our own production company—discovering, launching, and managing both solo artists and bands. Among them were four flamboyant young musicians who called themselves, of all things, Queen.

This is the story of those fifteen years, the music, the personalities and the moments that passed through those same doors, from John Lennon to Freddie Mercury.

It's a story that will—I hope—shine a light on a time and a place and a rock 'n' roll industry that has long gone. And I hope it will bring to life a world which every now and again—in Freddie's own words—was guaranteed to blow your mind . . .

One

In And Out Of The Shadows

"So what are we going to do? Cliff said. Shall we learn some of my songs? Don't need to, I said. We've done 'em all."

I hadn't always pictured myself as the owner of a recording studio—far from it. For a while I'd harboured dreams of being a pop star, not an engineer. I even achieved it. Well, sort of . . .

I'd wanted to be a drummer since I was an eight-year-old growing up in Cheshunt Hertfordshire a few miles outside London. I can still remember the day it hit me. My parents had taken my brother Barry and me to see a circus in Haringey Arena in North London. Sitting there inside the arena I'd been left cold by the lions and tigers, the trapeze artists, and the white-faced clowns. Instead I couldn't take my eyes off the drummer, knocking out a rhythm on the giant kit in the circus band. To me, it looked like the coolest thing in the world. I just knew I wanted to be a drummer too which was easier said than done, of course!

It was the early 50s, and money was scarce in post-war Britain. My parents certainly didn't have much, especially as my Dad had just started his own business. So I started saving up all I could from my milk and paper rounds and, in time with help from my dad, I got a cheap second hand drum kit. I spent every spare minute I had belting the hell out of it in our front room. (We had great neighbours.) By the time I was in my late teens I was pretty good, even if I say so myself. I started playing in a dance band, then graduating to traditional jazz and blues bands.

In 1959 I joined up with a local group run by a talented violinist turned guitarist named Brian Parker. They had been known originally as the Parker Royal Five, but were later rechristened The Hunters. The band was made up of me, Brian, Norman Stracey on rhythm guitar, John Rogers on bass, and Buster Meikle on vocals. We were semi-pro, juggling our day jobs with playing at local dance halls and sports clubs. But slowly we built up more work.

In August 1959 a local company called Abbey Recorders asked us to work on their stand at the Radio Show at Earls Court London. During this time the first stereo machines for home use began rolling out. We recorded some tracks live on stage, which the Abbey Recorder's people played back to the audience in order to demonstrate how good the machines were. It was a hint of what was to come for me, although I didn't know it at the time.

But then, in February 1960, we got our big break.

It started when we received a telegram, which was an event in itself. It arrived, addressed to the band via a guy called Len Bentley, who ran our local record shop in Waltham Cross. It was from Cliff Richard.

At the time, Cliff was the UK's answer to Elvis Presley and Britain's biggest star by a distance. There were others trying to compete— Marty Wilde and Tommy Steel in particular—but they weren't enjoying the sort of success that Cliff was getting. Cliff had broken through with his first hit "Move It" in 1958 and, with his backing band The Shadows, was selling records by the truckload.

Cliff was actually a neighbour of ours and a close friend of Brian's. He had grown up in Cheshunt too and had gone to the local secondary school. Brian had played in a band called The Dick Teague Skiffle Group with Cliff, and had even been offered a place in his backing band early on. He'd reckoned Cliff was going down the wrong road with his Elvis-style rock 'n' roll music and stuck to Skiffle. Bad call.

We were also linked through the local boys club where we often played, and where Cliff was known as the it's patron. He did a lot of charity work for the club and we often appeared on the same shows with him.

Anyhow, he'd sent the cable from America and wanted to know if The Hunters were available to be his backing band for a couple of gigs in London in a week's time.

The cable didn't say much more. Len told us that Cliff was touring America at the time but had to come back to honour these two commitments. He couldn't bring the Shadows with him because the union rules on foreign musicians in those days would only allow a straight swap. If four guys came in from a country then four guys could go out from here. That was the way it worked. If an American band came here, an English band had to go over there. Because Cliff's gigs were happening over one night, however, they couldn't send one of our bands over to the States for one night only. So he had to find a replacement backing band. His manager, the late Tito Burns, wanted to use some members of the Oh Boy! TV show band, but Cliff insisted on choosing his own musicians.

Our reaction to the cable was pretty instant. We said, "yeah, of course," even though we didn't know what the gigs were.

I asked my boss for some time off. Fortunately he was supportive and he agreed. We tried to send a telegram back to Cliff. We wanted to know what songs he was going to do. We knew he'd do "Living Doll" and that he'd have to do a twenty-five-minute act. But beyond that we knew nothing. I'd check every day with Len at the record store but there was nothing. So we got together one night and decided that the only thing we could do was to learn all his tunes—every single one of them.

He'd had one album and six singles (with B-sides) at that point in his career. We learned the whole frigging lot. We spent bloody hours on them, but it paid off.

Through Cliff's management we eventually got to know a bit more about the gigs we'd been hired for. When we did we nearly fell off our chairs. Cliff had to make two appearances in the same day. The first was at the annual NME music poll awards being held at the Wembley Arena. Also on the bill would be Gene Vincent and Eddie Cochran. The second was to collect a gold record for "Living Doll"—again live on television, this time at the London Palladium. That performance was going out live on TV's biggest show at the time, Sunday Night At The London Palladium hosted by Bruce Forsyth. The last time Cliff had played there with The Shadows they'd pulled an audience of twenty million people! Talk about being thrown in at the deep end.

It was the most intense week of my young life, I was twenty years old! We'd rehearsed every night, all week with Dave Sampson covering Cliff's vocals. Cliff arrived back in the UK at 10 p.m. Saturday night and came straight to us for a rehearsal. I can still picture it. We had a little rehearsal room set up in a prefab at the back of the school. Cliff turned up with his personal manager Ray Mackender.

"Nervous?" I asked Cliff, as we set up our gear.

"Slightly."

"So am I," I said

"So what are we going to do?" Cliff said. "Shall we learn some of my songs?"

"Don't need to," I said. "We've done 'em all."

He looked at me with a clear look of disbelief. So we played a couple of his tunes back for him and he just went "yeah, that's great." The hard work with Dave Sampson had paid off.

That weekend I hired a twelve-seater van from a hire firm in Enfield.

You weren't actually allowed to hire them for gigs. They thought rock 'n' roll people were hooligans—which in a way we were. The minute we got hold of this van we took most of the seats out so we could get all the gear in. The company would have gone nuts if they'd seen what we'd done to their van. But we didn't care. We were playing with Cliff Richard the following day. We were going to be pop stars.

We finished rehearsals at 2.30 in the morning on Sunday. At 8, just a few hours later, we had to leave for Central London for camera rehearsals at the Palladium. We would then head up to Wembley for the awards show and then go back down into Central London for the live show at the Palladium.

I picked Cliff up at his home in the morning. He only lived up the road. The mood in the van was a bit tense, although Cliff himself was great. People don't often realise it, but he's got a great sense of humour. I think he realised that, as inexperienced performers, we were beginning to realise the magnitude of what we were about to do. He kept our nerves at bay.

Getting set up for the gigs was knackering work. We weren't big enough to have any roadies or anything like that. We were carrying all our own gear. So we had to set it up at the Palladium for a camera and sound check. We left my drums there then drove back up to Wembley, where we'd made arrangements to use some of the Krew Kat's equipment, as they were backing Eddie Cochran.

When we got to Wembley we couldn't believe the audience. We were used to playing for three hundred people—tops. And that would be in a local cinema, sports club, or dance hall. But this was the Empire Pool itself, the most famous venue in the country. It was huge. There were ten thousand people there—most of them teenage girls.

To be honest, we were a bit star struck. We didn't want to do any work; we just wanted to watch the professionals, Gene Vincent and Eddie Cochran were huge then. I was still a twenty-year-old kid from England, and these guys were real legends to me. We'd been playing all their material for years. We wanted to hear how it should be played.

~

Cliff was due to be top of the bill, even though Gene Vincent and Eddie Cochran were also appearing. But, once we got to Wembley, it became clear that the running order would have to change to accommodate Cliff. The show was on in the afternoon and ran into the early evening. There was no way we were going to be able to close the show there, get de-rigged and get set up again in time at the Palladium, so it was decided that we'd close the first half of the show instead.

I was as nervous as hell before we went out onto the stage. The noise was unbelievable. As we started playing I couldn't hear a thing because ten thousand girls were all screaming, "We love Cliff!"

When we got going all I could hear was the bass drum. Fortunately we'd rehearsed everything to within an inch of its life and it all went fine. I didn't think it was possible, but as the set came to an end, the girls started screaming even louder than before. They weren't shouting for me or the rest of the band, of course. It was all for Cliff. But I felt a sense of satisfaction at having pulled it off in front of ten thousand kids.

We didn't have any time to dwell on what we'd done though, because we had to get straight back in the van and head into Central London. As we approached the theatre off Regent Street we saw kids hanging around the Palladium waiting for a glimpse of Cliff. They had no idea he was arriving in an anonymous grey van. So we pulled up outside the Palladium and unloaded him through the back door. No one even saw him.

We had a couple of hours' break after setting up, so we decided to relax and have a pint across the road at a pub. We thought it would calm our nerves a bit. But when we came out we got a hell of a shock.

I looked at the van. It was a brand new, light grey covered van— and it was absolutely covered in lipstick! Somehow the fans had sussed that this was Cliff's transport. They'd used their lipsticks to write WE LOVE CLIFF in block capitals right across the windscreen. I didn't have time to clear it off then. It would have to wait until the end of the concert.

~

Appearing on Sunday Night At the London Palladium was just about the biggest thing you could do as a performer then. To this day The Palladium is the most famous musical theatre of its kind in the world, and the variety show that beamed live every week was one of the most watched programmes on the telly. Eighteen million people tuned in every week to watch the show, which was hosted by Bruce Forsyth. You'd have had to play at Live Aid to beat that for an audience. It has been said that playing on stage at the London Palladium changes your life forever, and that was certainly true in our case!

Again, I didn't let the size of the TV audience get into my head as we backed Cliff for his twenty minute act including "Living Doll." The audience was a bit more subdued than the one at Wembley, though there was still a fair amount of screaming.

The show always ended the same way—with all the acts that had appeared that night standing on a roundabout which rotated on the giant stage. As the last act of the night we were there in place when the roundabout started turning. The only problem was that the riggers hadn't quite got it right and my drum kit started to swing around. At one point it looked as if it was going to cross the joints between the revolving part of the stage and the static part. That would have been interesting—falling off the roundabout in front of eighteen million people. But we managed to keep the kit on for the last couple of minutes while the show came to a close.

Afterwards there were congrats all round. Cliff was really complimentary about what we'd done. But again we didn't have time to get too big headed about it. We had to pack up and get the van filled up. I also had to get the lipstick cleared off, which proved a lot more difficult than I'd imagined since the girls had put the lipstick on sideways. So, I had to drive back home looking through a windscreen that was still smeared in a greasy film of pink lipstick. It got even worst when I made the mistake of putting the wipers on!

There was a little bit of press coverage about our performance in the following morning's papers. One local paper wrote, "The Hunters Came Through With Flying Colours." But to be honest, it hadn't really sunk in that we'd been playing to half the population of the UK the previous night. That soon changed as the day wore on.

When I took the van back to the guy in Enfield he caught me by surprise.

"Good show last night?" he said.

I just kind of shuffled around and mumbled. I didn't know what to say. How the hell did he know we'd played a show the previous night?

"By the way you're not allowed to hire a van for band jobs," he added, his face breaking into a smile. He went on, "You were very good on the telly by the way. Mind you, the old van was in a bit of a state last night."

Now he'd really got me going.

"How'd you know?"

"Because I followed you all the way back from Camden Town."

It turned out that by complete coincidence he'd been driving back at the same time. He'd followed us all the way back towards Enfield.

For a moment I thought we were for the high jump. Whatever money we'd made from the previous night was about to be blown on extra charges for the van.

But he just winked at me and waved me away.

"You did a bloody good job cleaning it up," he said.

Later that week we got a phone call from Cliff's agent, Tito Burns.

He was a straight shooting character, blunt and direct to the point: "Would you guys like to turn pro? You're good enough."

"Well, yeah," I thought to myself. But first I told Tito I'd better talk to the other guys.

We all rang each other up and had a quick chat.

We all had ordinary jobs. John Rogers was an office clerk, Norman Stracey worked in insurance and Brian worked at the local Dunlop factory. I was working as a coachbuilder. It was a solid job, but not exactly exciting. The chance of a full time music career seemed too good to miss. We all decided to give it a go.

So I went to work the next day to give in my notice. I'd been working for quite a big company, and my dad even knew the owner. So I thought I'd better go and see him.

I walked in, and before I could say anything he said, "Hello Norman, obviously you don't want to come back to work."

This was Tuesday morning. We'd had Monday off.

"Saw you on telly with Cliff on Sunday night. You were very good. Are you going to do it for real?" he asked.

"Yes, we are," I said.

"Well good luck, but if doesn't work out you've always got a job here," he said.

Which was really cool of him. He was a lovely bloke.

So we turned pro. Tito said he'd take us on and started giving us work. At first things started happening at a real rate of knots. Some months before we'd turned pro, we teamed up with a really good local singer called Dave Sampson. He was more reliable than Dave(Buster) Meikle and had a great voice. In many ways he was a better singer than Cliff, and he had the looks too. We thought he would be the element that would really break us into the big time.

The music business was still very much based on live performances at dance halls and clubs at that point. Our first job was a little mini tour of the Southampton and Bournemouth area. We went to work for a guy called Len Cannon, who used to own a famous ballroom down there. It was a real education for us. We were stuck in terrible digs that were full of down-and-outers and tramps and the gigs weren't exactly brilliant either. We'd play to kids at the cinema in the mornings then to a different audience in the afternoons and evenings. But we learned our first valuable lessons. For a start, we learned we should always book our own accommodations whenever we went on tour from then on.

It wasn't long before we secured a recording contract with EMI. Dave Sampson was largely responsible for landing the deal. Dave was our Cliff, and he sounded a bit like him too. He was a talented guy and could write as well. At one point Dave showed Cliff a song that he'd written on the back of a restaurant menu. It was called "Sweet Dreams". He'd been really nervous when he'd gone round to Cliff's house, but Cliff had been really gracious and given it a listen. His reaction had been immediate. He said, "I love this, stay there, don't go anywhere." He then jumped on his Lambretta motor scooter and drove round to see his producer Norrie Paramor. Cliff apparently quite fancied the song for himself, but Norrie said "let the kid record it himself," and Cliff finally agreed. He shot back to the house where Dave was still waiting and broke the good news. The next day Norrie offered Dave and The Hunters a recording deal. We were on our way.

We went into the EMI studios at Abbey Road towards the end of March in 1960 and recorded "Sweet Dreams" as our first single. I can still remember the strange atmosphere when we walked into Studio 2, which of course later became famous for the Beatles' recordings. It was the size of an aircraft hangar and had all the atmosphere of one. The studio felt like an electrical laboratory, with loads of bespectacled blokes in long, white coats and clipboards. You also couldn't do anything to alter the sound or volume without asking someone's permission. It was a real creative straitjacket, although when I look back on it we enjoyed many sessions there, either with Dave or as session players for EMI's many other artists. In the end, the conditions may not have been ideal, but we were learning our craft.

~

Despite the studio conditions, we made a pretty good record, one that had the potential to make Dave—and the rest of us—stars. It all started well. We were booked to go on Oh Boy! to promote it, and early sales were strong. We entered the charts in May 1960 at No. 29 and were expected to go much higher, especially with the clout of EMI behind us. But then something strange happened: EMI ran out of copies. How did that happen? How could the biggest music company in the country be unable to meet demand for a record? That was their bread and butter. Easy. It's a question I still ask myself to this day. And I think I know the answer. The reality was that the record business was very tightly controlled then. EMI saw Dave and us as potential rivals to their big act, Cliff Richard and the Shadows. I think Cliff's team had signed us as a way of keeping an eye on us in order to make sure we didn't pose too big a threat to their golden boy.

Looking back on it, there were lots of other clues that we weren't going to get too far. In November 1961, for instance, we got a letter from the then all-powerful Grade Organisation and one of its chief promoters, a guy called Arthur Howes. He booked a lot of bands for TV pop shows and concerts, and had the ability to really push the groups he worked with. We did TV shows like Cliff's Spectacular, Saturday Special, the Wham Show, as well as a string of tours backing people like Bobby Rydell, Jimmy Jones, Craig Douglas, Michael Cox, Frank Ifield, Ronnie Carroll, Kenny Lynch, Mark Wynter and the Allisons.

In the letter Arthur wrote us, he said that the Grade Organisation couldn't use us on a couple of Sunday concerts that were coming up because there would be "too much of a clash with The Shadows." He was happy to use us as a backing band for other artists, but as Dave Sampson and The Hunters we had a limited future.

It was frustrating because we weren't attempting to copy The Shads at all. But that was the problem. We were seen as a rival to the Shadows.

At that point, however, I wasn't too upset about it. My ambition at that stage was to be a good pro and have a good time. I think I achieved both those things.

We carried on working hard. We did three or four Cliff television specials, travelling around the country to appear with him. We did the Wham shows, which was similar to the Oh Boy! and Boy Meets Girl shows. Then we landed a three-month summer season in Bournemouth, where we helped open a new theatre at the end of the pier. The compére was Ted Rogers. Across the road was Shirley Bassey doing her own show at the Pavilion. It was an exciting time, and we did some wild things.

We were being paid £55 a week for the Bournemouth gigs as the house band, which was a lot of money when you consider the average wage at the time was around £10 a week. I managed to save enough money for a deposit on a new station wagon for the band. I was the only driver at the time, and I virtually wore the thing out over the next few years.

For a while we were a backing band for all and sundry. We also did stuff for the well-known producer Joe Meek, recording in his place on Holloway Road with Mike Cox, Danny Rivers, and others. We auditioned for the BBC's Saturday Club, which Brian Matthews presented on a Saturday morning.

The money was very good. But we still weren't breaking through in the way we'd hoped.

The suspicion that we'd been signed to make sure we didn't pose too big a threat to Cliff Richard and the Shadows continued to grow as time went by.

In October 1961, Tito Burns wrote to say that he couldn't act as our sole agent. He was struggling to get us work in some areas, again because the feeling was that we were too similar to The Shads.

Just like with EMI, I think he signed us up because he thought we were a threat to The Shadows. We'd shown we could do it. We were making a lot of noise in the street.

Our reputation as session musicians was pretty well established by now. We'd recorded singles with Mike Cox, Tony Eden, Tony Brent, Cherry Wainer, and Roy Young. Norrie Paramor's number two, John Schroeder, went to Fontana—another popular label—and invited us to record for them just as The Hunters. Of course, we were still recording with Dave Sampson on the EMI label, so this was a similar deal to the one that The Shadows had. They recorded independently from Cliff as well as part of Cliff Richard and The Shadows.

~

We had a small instrumental hit with a song called "Teen Scene", which funny enough came back again when it featured in the award-winning movie An Education in 2009.

We also cut our first album.

"Teen Scene" had done well enough to justify an album, which we recorded with a producer named Jack Baverstock. He was the kind of guy who wanted everything done at breakneck speed. He'd pick some hits out from the chart and get us to knock out a cover version in one take. It wasn't ideal—in fact it was far from it.

For the cover of the album some bright spark had the idea of dressing us in pith helmets standing over a dead tiger! We were The Hunters, after all.

To get this shot, they took us out to the Royal Forest Hotel in Chingford one freezing cold winter's morning. There were a couple of locals out walking. They looked at us as if we were completely off our rockers. Strangely enough, the album is now a collector's item!

During this time we also did a lot of backing work for artists at Fontana. We did sessions, broadcasts, and gigs. We were on good money, very good money.

One of the bonuses was that we could all read music. When the big, American entertainer and singer Bobbie Rydell came over union rules prevented him from bringing his band with him. So we were hired to back him. He was a great American entertainer. He could play sax and sing.

We had six weeks on the road with him. That was fun. We also backed another American named Jimmy Jones, who had a big hit with "Handyman". We were on the road with him for weeks. But it wasn't really happening for us as a chart act.

Our last throw of the dice was with a single called "The Storm", which we'd written—funny enough—during a thunderstorm one night while we were rehearsing at the Cheshunt Boys Club. We'd come up with the idea of an instrumental that used electric guitars and sound effects to echo the drama of thunder and lightning. But when Brian sneaked a Watkins Copycat echo unit into the studio, our Fontana producer Jack Baverstock banned him from using it.

That was proof to me again that the big, corporate studios were stifling creativity. This incident planted the seed of an idea that would come to fruition some years later.

Despite the studio's attempts to spoil the song, "The Storm" showed every sign of being a hit and was on target to hit the charts—and the upper reaches too. We'd been booked to play on The Saturday Club on the BBC, and Fontana had been doing a lot of behind the scenes string pulling. If we'd trusted the record company a bit more it might have all panned out. But we didn't—and that was the root of our downfall.

We'd been let down before by EMI and didn't want a repeat of what had happened with "Sweet Dreams". We were determined to do everything we could to help the single along and had enlisted every friend and contact we had to order the single at record shops all over London. We'd also gotten people to send a massive number of postcards to The Saturday Club asking them to play "The Storm". Unfortunately the BBC was really worried at the time about the dodgy side of the record industry, the "payola" thing where companies paid stations to play their records. Someone at the BBC smelled a non-existent rat and pulled us from The Saturday Club. That was that. "The Storm" fizzled out.

It was a blow, but to be honest, by that stage—late 1962—I had pretty much realised I wasn't going to be a pop star. For a start, I had a feeling that the old days of variety-based acts like us were numbered. We'd scraped around at the bottom of the charts and had a few sniffs of success, but nothing significant. Our band didn't have a stage act as such. We were very good musicians, but at that time the audience wanted to see everyone leaping around doing their thing. The Shadows had their dancing act, which they "borrowed" from the American band The Treniers. They had it off to a T though. But a wind of change was about to blow through the business soon anyway, so perhaps it was all for the best.

My life was changing quite dramatically too. By now I'd met and married my girlfriend Chris. We'd married in September 1961 and then had our first child in 1962. So I had responsibilities, mouths to feed. I felt it wasn't really right to be still on the road with a wife and a child.

The night the writing on the wall really revealed itself came when, again in 1962, we drove the van up to Liverpool to play in a place called the Cavern Club. It's taken on legendary status since then, but back then it didn't have much going for it—at all. It was exactly what it said on the tin—a cavern-like space underneath the street. To be honest, it was a bit of a dump.

We were topping the bill that night. Supporting us was a band called Tony Sheridan and The Beat Boys. They had apparently been working the clubs in Hamburg up in Germany and had picked up a bit of a following over there. They'd had all sorts of personnel and name changes over the years. People had come and gone. I didn't really pay them that much attention, to tell the truth. But they had a look that was slightly different, sort of beatnik like. I'd like to say I saw something in the three guys in the band who were driving the thing along, supporting Tony Sheridan. But I've got no memory of George Harrison, Paul McCartney, and John Lennon. I think I was too focused on getting through our gig in one piece and getting the hell out of there and Liverpool.

It wouldn't be long, however, before the three backing players from the Cavern would start turning the music business on its head. The good news for me was that I'd be one of the beneficiaries of the revolution they were about to begin.

Two

Into The Alley

" That's it, I said to Barry. What's what? he said, unsure what I was on about. The name of the studio. Trident. "

The crumbling interior of the building was like something out of a Dickens novel. I half expected to find Oliver Twist and the Artful Dodger hiding in the shadows.

As I walked through the door and stepped inside the dark and dusty entrance, the air was filled with the smell of damp and stale urine. It looked as if someone had ripped the place apart. There were bare walls and exposed floors, lead acid tanks, a furnace, and cables and trunking hanging down everywhere. It had been an old engraving works. It was a bloody sorry sight—but it was exactly what I was looking for.

"This is perfect," I said to myself.

It was November 1966, and I'd been scouring the streets of Soho for what now seemed like an age looking for the right premises. There was no internet in the 1960s and I couldn't face mailing a load of estate agencies, so I'd decided that I'd wear out some shoe leather and do the job on foot. I was a man on a mission.

After a few days marching around the alleyways south of Oxford Street, however, I was beginning to regret it. I must have looked at a dozen buildings with "To Let" signs on them, but none of them fitted the bill. But then I'd been told about this disused building in St. Anne's Court, a narrow alleyway between Dean Street and Wardour Street. The moment I saw it I sensed my search was over. I just knew it was the right place to build a recording studio, and not just any recording studio, the best in London—or anywhere else for that matter.

~

The seeds of the idea of building a world-class recording studio had been sewn a few years earlier. By the end of 1963 The Hunters' career had ground to a halt. The band had gone their separate ways. The Beatles had arrived and the whole world was changing, clearly we didn't fit into the new order that was taking shape. So with my career as a pop star over and a growing family to feed, I'd decided to take a step in a more solid and reliable direction and buy a local record and musical instrument shop.

By coincidence my mother-in-law had a radio and TV retail shop with a record department. Chris and I decided to buy it, thinking we would convert it into a record and musical instrument store. I'd opened the store on the High Street near the new home I'd built with my wife Chris, in Broxbourne. Even after opening the music shop, though, I still had a deep feeling in my gut that if I changed tack I could still make money in the record business.

We got off to a good start. I was known locally, so our shop was well supported by local musicians. We hired my brother Barry, who was employed locally as a television repairman. Chris and I also got involved in local music promotions. We ended up running four dance halls on various nights of the week, and were booking major acts like Georgie Fame, The Who, The Animals, and The Honeycombs. This allowed me to let local bands be the support acts, and in turn generated more business for our shop.

I do remember our telephone being cut off one time. I knew the bill had been paid so I phoned the telephone company from the pub next door, only to be told by the telephone supervisor that our phone had been disconnected because we were playing music over the line! I pointed out in no uncertain terms that music was very likely to come over our telephone, we were a bloody record shop!

How times have changed.

It was a golden period for record shops. The record retail business was booming, in large part thanks to The Beatles. But I'd also begun to use the place as a recording studio, inviting local bands—and other contacts I'd made in the music business—to lay down some tracks there. Also at the time I had been commissioned to write the music for several commercials with Brian Parker, including gigs for the Ford Motor Company, Max Factor, and Mary Quant.

The latter was for a seven-minute epic film called Youthquake that we recorded at CTS studio. The band comprised Gerry Salisbury on bass, Brian Parker on guitar, myself on drums, and John Lord (later of Deep Purple) on Hammond Organ.

I was doing well. Between the success of the shop and the promotions business, Barry and I had been able to develop our interest in the recording studio side of the business quite easily.

Slowly but surely we had acquired some quality second hand equipment, including a couple of stereo tape machines and parts for a mixing desk. We had set up the control room in the upstairs office and created the "studio" downstairs in the shop, where the musicians did their stuff after hours. The sight of bands belting out songs in a shop window on the High Street in the middle of the night used to amuse the passers-by to no end. But we didn't care. We were opening the door into a new world of possibilities.

By 1966 we'd taken the studio as far as we could, however. By this stage we had some great equipment in there, including a secondhand state-of-the-art Ampex 2-track recorder. But the simple fact was that we didn't have enough space. We'd outgrown the place as far as recording was concerned. If we were going to go any further with it we needed to move to better premises. And we had to think big— bigger than anything we'd tried before.

I knew in my bones it was the right thing to do, but there were still plenty of hurdles to overcome.

At first I planned to stay local and had my eye on an ABC Bakers building across the road from the shop. It was a huge place with a dance hall at the back, complete with a lovely herringbone floor that had been laid for the era of tea dances in the 1940s and 1950s.

I thought we could convert it into a studio, but the landlord would only give us a nine-month lease, which didn't fit with our plans at all. We were in it for the long haul.

When that fell through, my mind turned to the West End and at that time a lot of the big recording facilities were based outside Central London. Decca were in Hampstead, Philips at Stanhope Place, Pye at Great Cumberland Place, and EMI, of course, at

Abbey Road. There were a few small independents around, most notably IBC in Portland Place opposite the BBC, and Tin Pan Alley Studios and Regent Sound in Denmark Street. But there wasn't an independent music studio in the heart of "Musicland" in Soho.

The area was the creative hub of London. Since the 1950s and earlier, the music business had been centred around Denmark Street and Tin Pan Alley, as it was known. All the musicians met on the Nearby Archer Street, which was also the base of the powerful Musicians Union. Film companies were based around Wardour Street, and the adjoining streets were full of clubs, musical instrument shops, and other arty hangouts. The energy of the place was becoming irresistible. Carnaby Street and the fashion scene was a short walk away as well. The place really was the epicentre of Swinging Sixties London.

Which was exactly why I'd started tramping day after day around the West End while Chris and Barry continued to run the shop, providing us with a source of income. And it was why I knew I'd struck gold when I saw the unlikely-looking building in St. Anne's Court.

I got in contact with my brother Barry and asked him to have a look at the building as well. He was going into business with me, so it was important I had his backing. He agreed it was in a great location and had almost limitless potential. I couldn't have agreed more. The more I looked at the building the more it felt artistically right. It turned out the building had been the home of the West End Engraving Company and, according to some locals, had previously been a Victorian bakery. It was a place where—for a century or more—men had done intricate, creative work. That had to be a good sign, I told myself.

A couple of days after first seeing the place I went to see the landlords, Sir Richard Sutton Settled Estates, about renting the building and its 7,500 square feet. The space was bigger than we actually needed, but I had a plan to sublet some of the surplus space to make some extra cash.

The owners were real gentleman landlords who worked out of a building over on Curzon Street. Their offices were all wood panelling and leather. You could almost smell the old money. They inhabited another world completely. Would they even agree to let the building to a small start-up? Having explained what a recording studio was and did through the course of several meetings, they agreed to let the building to us. They also agreed to a period of six months' rent-free occupation whilst we carried out the necessary construction and cleared the place out. When the full rent kicked in we'd pay £6 a square foot.

The landlords actually liked some of the plans we had for the place, in particular my idea of putting a lift in. They weren't quite so sure about my idea about ripping up the ground floor in order to create a double room-height studio—with a studio at basement level and the control room on the ground floor level above it. They definitely raised a few eyebrows at that. Reluctantly they agreed, but on one condition: at the end of the lease they said the ground floor would have to go back in, which I agreed to. I had to if I was going to achieve the things I wanted with the studio. I had big plans.

From the outset, I knew that two things were crucial if this venture was going to succeed. First, we had to go for broke and create something big. But I also knew it had to be a place that encouraged musicians to be creative.

The way the music industry was back then, everything was a question of economics. The number one rule of recording was to keep the record company's cost at rock bottom. That meant that bands were only allowed to record an album when they were note perfect. Musicians would rehearse for sometimes months in advance and then head to the studio for the shortest possible time. It was in many ways a throwback to the old days of musical theatre and variety. Recording studios were originally places where famous stage acts would record their best-known performances for posterity. They'd walk in and perform as if they were at the Palladium. It was a case of in, out, and bosh. But that didn't really apply to modern bands like The Beatles who, with their producer George Martin, were experimenting with all sorts of new possibilities in recording. That was where my opportunity lay.

The way I saw it, the old-style studio had no respect for creative work, for improvising, for getting lucky with something at the last minute. I thought making music should be a looser process.

To achieve that, I was also determined to create an atmosphere that was different from what were regarded as the "top studios", the places that we humble musicians were encouraged to think of as shrines to the perfect recording. Don't get me wrong: those studios were technically clever, but my god were they soul-destroying places in which to work. It wasn't just the atmosphere that was cold and clinical. These places were populated by an alien race—The White-Coated Engineers and The Brown-Coated Maintenance Men. These were laboratories without soul, and without any time for artists to develop their talents.

What my brother Barry and I had in mind was the exact polar opposite of that.

With the keys to the building in St. Anne's Court in my hand, I began to visualise the studio that I was going to create. For a while my wife Chris and I were forced to sleep in a bedroom that was covered in huge, A1 sized drawings. I began to eat, sleep—and dream—about the studio I wanted to create.

The idea of having a set up where the control room was on a different level to the artists was already central to my thinking. It had worked at the shop—more by accident than design. I wanted to do the same thing here, create a situation where the artist and the producer weren't staring each other in the eye all the time. I knew from personal experience that this was intimidating and restricting for performers. I wanted to give the artist more space, both literally and psychologically.

Some people thought—and continue to think—that it was a bit of a goldfish bowl to have the technicians peering down on the musicians, but that's how it was at Abbey Road and IBC studios as well. I thought their argument was rubbish—and fortunately a lot of others shared my view.

The other thing I knew would be crucial was the acoustics of the studio. So I got the top acoustic designer at the BBC, Sandy Brown, to help with the design of the place.

He was based not too far away, above the St. George's Hotel where the BBC had offices. We'd decamp to the BBC Green Room, where over a beer or scotch or two we planned the studio.

We went for a mix of the traditional "Live Room" and "Dead Room", with most of the studio carpeted to absorb sound and a small, "live" end to the room furnished with polished cork tiles. With a structural engineer named John Spelzine, we started putting together some costings.

It was all ambitious, cutting edge stuff. And it wasn't cheap. So I knew that we weren't going to get anywhere without some money— serious money—behind us. I reckoned we needed to raise around £55,000 (c.£850,000)—to get the work we needed done.

So the first thing we needed to do was sell the old record shop and studio. I sold the shop in January 1967 to the Wimpy Bars Hamburger franchise. All the interior fittings were snapped up by two guys who had a Caribbean music shop in Soho, David Betteridge and Chris Blackwell. The pair also had a fledgling music label, Island Records, which would do quite well for itself a few years later. By now I had two sons, Darren and Russell, so I had to think carefully about my family. But, with my wife Chris's blessing, I re-mortgaged the house we'd built for ourselves a couple of years earlier and raised £13,000. My brother Barry who had no money of his own re-mortgaged our parent's family home and so was able to invest £7,000 into the studio. Even with this money, we were still way short of what we needed.

Luckily a mate of mine named David Gillard knew of an investment company in London, Dunbar Securities, who'd recently put money into the commercial production company known as MRM Productions, for which he was a director. It turned out some members of the landed gentry ran the investment company, Michael Jardine-Paterson and David Hope Dunbar. I met them and their MD Robert Iggulden, who expressed an interest in investing in the studio. We closed the deal on a piece from a note book in a cafe across the road from the premises that I hoped would soon be mine. In the end, Dunbar Securities agreed to put up £35,000, the balance we needed to start converting the place. Dunbar even extracted a seven thousand pound investment from his mother to help us convert the upper stories of the building into offices.

The deal was that Michael had the controlling shares of the new company. He'd give them back to us when we made our first fifty thousand in profit. Taking a conservative view, he gave us five years in which to do that. He would soon be surprised at just how conservative that estimate was.

And so it was that we started what would be a twelve-month process—converting the disused old building into a state-of-the-art recording studio, with an accompanying film preview theatre fit for both film and rock 'n' roll royalty.

We hired our first employees: Jerry Salisbury, an old friend and a renowned brass and bass player; Bernie Smith, a really talented carpenter, who, like Jerry, stayed with us for years; and Ron Goodwin, a maintenance engineer, and Dave Bazley. It was left to the six of us to strip the building and begin the re-construction of a five thousand square foot building.

As time moved on we hired some more muscle in the form of friends, including two brothers named Bill and David Hole and Dave Bazeley. Bill and Dave would also remain at Trident as a regular member of the team. We also hired a construction company to carry all of the structural works needed, the installation of a lift, the removal of the ground floor, a new staircase to the studio, the construction of toilets, and all sorts of other work.

~

The process was far from straightforward and had more than its fair share of incidents.

The sound quality inside the building was obviously crucial. So when, one quiet day, we heard the sound of heavy machinery whirring away next door, we panicked. It turned out the place next door was home to some rostrum cameras owned by Rank that were bolted to the adjoining wall and making it vibrate. So we had no choice but to build a false wall, two inches inside the original.

Then, while we were digging out the shaft that would carry our lift, we came across a big old sewer drain. We asked the council permission to remove it and they instructed us to "break it in half and see what happens." We did so with a small gang of Irish labourers. When we split the drain open rats the size of small dogs starting scurrying out. The Irishmen made quick work of them, however, by flattening them out with their spades. Thank God we had them there.

As the building took shape, there were plenty of funny moments like that. On another occasion we were constructing a lift shaft through the building. The roof had been removed and the top of the building was covered in tarpaulin.

One morning following several days of rain, one of the workers pulled back the tarp cover without thinking, and inadvertently dumped several dozen gallons of water down the lift shaft, straight onto two of his Irish workmates who were in the bottom at the time. One emerged like a drowned rat, hat plastered close to his head and his clothes sticking to him, shovel in hand, looking for the bastard that was up on the roof. We saw what had happened and made a quick exit to another part of the building to stifle our laughter.

The building comprised some five thousand square feet between the studio, the theatre, and the top two floors, which were to be fitted out and let short-term. The finish was to be a white plastic finished wallboard.

I decided to buy the whole lot in one go, thereby getting a discount.

Unfortunately when delivery day arrived I stepped into Wardour Street to be confronted by an articulated truck about ten feet high and forty feet long, crammed with boarding.

"Which bit is ours?" I asked.

"The lot Guv," he said.

I crept back to the studio and told the six guys inside to give me a hand.

When they saw the truck they were not pleased to say the least, as there were hundreds of boards, each six feet by two feet and weighing about pounds.

I knew we had to get the lot off that day so I went and saw Sid, the landlord of the Ship Pub next door, to borrow his barrel barrow.

We could get about eight boards on each trip up the alley behind the Ship and into the front door.

It took over eight hours to move the lot into the studio, and we burnt out the bearings on on Sid's barrow in the process.

We finished up with this huge pile of plasterboard. As we were leaving that night I asked Barry whether he knew what the floor loading was. I reckoned this lot weighed ten tons.

"Well, we're going to take the floor out anyway," he joked unhelpfully.

I did not sleep that night.

~

As the infrastructure of the building took shape, so too did the studio, although again we had our fair share of teething troubles.

As far as the equipment side of things was concerned, my philosophy was simple: I wanted the best and I wanted to offer facilities that no one else could match.

I'd fallen in love with the second-hand Ampex stereo machine we'd had at the shop. We'd bought it from IBC studios in London. So, with Barry, I headed out to the Ampex Reading office to see the latest equipment in the Ampex range. I came back having ordered a mono machine, a stereo machine, a 4-track machine and—the piece de resistance—an as yet unseen 8-track machine. It would be the first of its kind in Europe!

I headed back from Reading to Soho feeling very excited. I knew the 8-track would put us ahead of the game right away. Even EMI didn't have an 8-track. All that was left to do now was the small matter of paying for it all.

Fortunately, after much persuasion—and many hours explaining the technicalities of 8-track recording to a baffled finance executive— we got funding from Lombard.

The most expensive item of the lot, however, was the mixing desk, which would be the hub of our recording operation. Again we wanted the best. I had heard people praising a company called Sound Techniques, who had a studio in Old Church Street, Chelsea. They built their own desks and had recorded people like The Pink

Floyd, Fairport Convention, and Jethro Tull. We ordered one of their "A Range" desks. It was only when it was about to be delivered that I realised it came in a steel and aluminium frame. I hated it. It reminded me of the monstrous machines you found at the BBC or EMI. I wanted our studio to feel softer, warmer, and less robotic than that. So I asked Lockwood, the company that was making our speakers—again top of the range —to create a teak veneer outer casing for the desk.

It cost a bomb, of course, but it looked great when it was finally installed. I have to admit that we didn't set many clothing trends in Swinging Sixties London, but my mixing desk did kick start a new fashion. Walk into most studios today and that's what you'll find there—a wooden frame around the mixing desk. Perhaps I should have patented the idea!

We were determined to be innovative as a studio. So, unlike most standard studios, we decided to place our recording machines in a separate room, away from the artists. We had two trains of thought here: first we wanted to remove the distraction of the tape machines turning over while the musicians were playing, and secondly we wanted to reduce the number of bodies in the studio. Therefore we built the machine room on the first floor where all the equipment could be controlled by remote.

It all worked pretty smoothly, that is, apart from the nights when we were haunted. It happened a couple of times during those early days, especially when the old building was quiet. Guys would come into the main studio white faced saying that it had "gone cold and spooky again." One musician, the drummer Steve Gadd, who played with the band Charlie, reckoned he met a ghost at the top of the building late one night. He refused to ever set foot in the building again.

~

We knew our operation needed to make a lot of money—and fast. Early on we'd decided to complete the top two floors of the building before anything else, partly with an eye on renting them out as offices. This had proved a prescient bit of thinking. Our friends at

MRM Productions had liked the look and location of the building and had taken the entire space as their offices.

But we'd also decided to build a preview theatre in the building. The logic here was simple. Long term we knew we'd want to work with sound and vision as a dubbing facility and perhaps making films to accompany singles as The Beatles were already doing. In the short term, however, we were right in the middle of the British film industry's backyard.

Straightaway we head hunted the film projectionist Dick Slade, who worked on Wardour Street and was recognised as the best in the UK. His black book would be invaluable. When he joined Trident we all realised what a great character and asset he would turn out to be. Dick always had the latest jokes to tell, and could soften up any difficult situation. Such was his character that he could deal one day with the likes of Michael Winner and the next host a birthday party for one of our children by showing a children's film. He also ran a mean bar.

It didn't prove too hard to spread the word and get people in. Among the first was the director Carl Foreman, who was soon using the theatre to watch the daily rushes for his film Mackenna's Gold with Gregory Peck and Omar Sharif.

~

Construction proved to be a slow and painful process. We completed the theatre first and opened it in November 1967. By early spring in 1968 we'd kitted out the studio and the rest of the building as well. All we had to do now was make sure it all worked.

Of course, it wasn't that simple. Nothing ever was.

With the fitting out of the studio almost complete, Sandy and I ran some tests. The traditional trick was to fire a starting pistol so that a sound engineer could check the time delay and take all sorts of other esoteric little measurements. We did this, but then Sandy turned to me and said "fuck all this, let's get some music in here." I couldn't have agreed more.

I hastily put together a jazz band with my friend Gerry Salisbury on bass, Roger Barnes on piano, Tony Horn on vocals, and yours truly on drums. I then got a seven-piece soul band in called Gonzales to belt out their stuff while we tested the equipment.

It sounded great—I guess it was always going to with Sandy Brown at the helm. We were so excited about what we'd achieve; but I was realistic enough to know it would be what others thought that really counted.

While the mono, stereo, and 4-track machines worked fine, the 8-track was another matter. It arrived about six weeks after we opened, one of only three of these machines in the world. Machine Number 2 had been installed at Atlantic Studios in New York. Machine Number 1 was at Ampex's headquarters in California. So there weren't too many people who'd worked with them—and more to the point, modified them.

When we first fitted the machine we discovered a fundamental problem—it was set up for US electrical mains, and not UK, they had shipped it with the wrong motors, and as a result it was running at the wrong speed. This oversight caused the 8-track to make everyone sound like Mickey Mouse, which of course was a complete and utter disaster.

Fixing the bloody machine proved a real nightmare. We exchanged telexes with Ampex in the USA who promised to send over suitable motors as quickly as possible but they had to be made for the UK market. In the meantime we were talking to the engineers at Atlantic Studios in New York who were also working out how to get the best sounds from this amazing new piece of equipment. We shared a lot of useful information that, I think, helped us both. Whilst waiting for the new motors to arrive, we found a piece of kit to solve the speed and pitch problem: an ex Army rheostat that allowed us to change the speed.

We knew that it wasn't a long-term solution. It wouldn't cause problems for people who recorded at Trident, but the masters could only be played on our equipment, at least until everyone else in the business had 8-track equipment of their own. But we weren't going to worry about that at that point. We were ready for business.

Before we opened, the project had been known as the "Sheffield Studio", which wasn't too great a name from a marketing point of view. It made sense, but it wasn't very exciting, and it didn't have a good ring to it. Then one day, after slogging our guts out in the building for another twelve hours or so, Barry and myself were walking along Wardour Street when there was a deafening roar overhead. We looked up and saw a plane lumbering over the streets of Soho, beginning its descent into Heathrow. I recognised the plane immediately as a Hawker Siddeley HS.121 passenger plane, more popularly known as "The Trident".

"That's it," I said to Barry.

"What's what?" he said, unsure what I was on about.

"The name of the studio. Trident."

It made sense on all sorts of levels. There were effectively three of us in the business: me, Barry, and our investors at Dunbar. There were three main strands to the business too: music recording, film recording, and the movie preview theatre.

To announce Trident's arrival on the scene, I worked with a designer on the creation of a Logo, the now famous Trident Triangle, and we put out a press release. Anyone reading it would have come to the conclusion that we were clearly hedging our bets on which part of our operation was going to be our core business. The release described how "record and film producers, advertising agents, production companies, etc. will have available under one roof the following facilities: film-recording, music-recording, disc-cutting, tape-copying, tape-reduction, as well as one of the best preview theatres in Wardour Street."

It also quoted me as saying, "For a long time there has been a crying need for a co-ordinated high speed service. Now producers and directors can come to us, tell us what they want, and we can plan the programme for them in the shortest possible time." I was twenty-eight years old, but not lacking in confidence. "I know that Trident can save them at least a third of the time it used to take on any job," I boasted. I was confident we could deliver on the promise, but still nervous, not least because we didn't yet have the clients to put everything to the test. That was the next piece in the jigsaw. We also produced what I think was the first ever studio published brochure, rate card and facility list, which caused some consternation in the recording industry.

One day I received a call from the chairman of the Recording Association, saying, "We don't advertise. It cheapens things."

"Why shouldn't you? Are you embarrassed about your prices and services?" I replied.

It was sour grapes. I knew we had services that they could not offer.

So, on the night of Friday March 8th, 1968, following a great deal of planning by Chris, my wife and other members of the team, we set up a bar and buffet in the main studio and another bar in the preview theatre. Our tenants MRM even set up a bar in their offices.

The place was heaving, with people spilling out into the alleyway and the street below. Many of the people who'd helped us get to the point rounded out the ample guest list.

Our investors Michael Jardine-Patterson, Sir David Hope-Dunbar and Robert Iggulden were there, knocking back champagne along with the rest of us. So too were all those who'd helped us equip and fit out the place (apart from the Irish rat-killer navvies, of course.) We were not serving Guinness that night !!

But as well as celebrating the end of a year's hard work in creating the studio, we wanted the party to be a shop window for what we could do. We needed customers.

Everyone wanted to know what the 8-track could do. "Does it actually work?" was the most common question.

"You'll have to book us to find out," was our usual reply.

We had hired Gonzales to come back and play live in the studio. We all drank a lot—carrying on until three in the morning. But the party turned up trumps in more ways than one. The music business was a small world, a village really. News and gossip spread fast. So it was no surprise that a lot of people came along to the party, mainly out of curiosity.

Among them was a young sound engineer called Malcolm Toft. At the time he was working for CBS, but earning peanuts. He was still living with his mum and dad in Kingston on Thames.

He'd heard about us through the grapevine, which wasn't surprising. There weren't many new, independent recording studios opening in London at the time. He'd also heard that we were looking for a new sound engineer.

It's all a bit hazy to me, but apparently he'd struck up a conversation with my brother Barry in the preview theatre. Barry had had a few drinks and just announced at the top of his voice: "Is anybody looking for a job?" Malcolm had gingerly put his hand up and started talking to him. He'd actually thought it would go nowhere, but three days later Barry had given him a call at CBS and asked him over to meet us. We'd given him a glass of red wine, asked him to do a mix for us on the desk, and hired him on the spot. He joined us in April 1968, and immediately become one of our main engineers.

The most useful short-term connection we made that night, however, was another engineer, Alan Oduffy, who worked at Olympic Studios. He was working with one of the biggest pop acts at the time, Manfred Mann. They'd had a series of hits since the mid-sixties with songs like "5-4-3-2-1" and "Do-Wah-Diddy", but had become a more substantial act in recent years with songs like "Pretty Flamingo" and a version of Bob Dylan's "The Mighty Quinn". That had just been a big No. 1 in the UK. So the pressure was on for them to follow that up with another hit.

The engineer said he'd recommend Manfred Mann use Trident for their next single. He was as good as his word and within days we'd had a call booking them in to the studio.

They recorded a song called "My Name Is Jack". It sounded inoffensive enough and we laid it down for them pretty easily. But just as it was about to be released, Mercury Records in the States objected to something in the lyrics and said it had to be changed. Fortunately, it didn't have too much of an impact on sales here—in fact it might have helped it. When it came out in the spring it went flying straight to the top of the heap.

We had our first No. 1 single. We were on the map.

~

Soho in the late sixties was a very colourful place—to put it mildly. The chap next door to us was called Harry and he ran a company that had been supplying haberdashery and buttons to the tailoring business for a hundred years. Above him was an even longer established business, in fact the oldest profession in the world. The call girls who worked on the first floor had windows that looked out on to ours. They weren't too bothered about drawing the curtains so we were often privy to seeing just how hard they worked for their money. It was quite a sight.

Across the road from us was another typical Soho establishment, a strip joint called Sun City. It was one of a string of places owned by a lady called Linda King.

She was another real character. She was a big bird with a fur coat. She'd come along each evening with two Borzoi dogs and a minder as she collected all the takings. It was hardly surprising that she was often on the wrong side of the law. I lost count of the number of times she had her collar felt by the cops. She'd always leave her dogs with local traders while she reported to Saville Row police station.

We struck up a good relationship with Linda. She was even good enough to lend us some of her girls, no charge, for the occasional quick show in the studio when a recording session wasn't going well and needed a bit of "livening up".

One day Chris was walking down St. Anne's Court with two of our boys when Linda came along with her dogs. They stopped and started chatting outside one of Linda's cinemas. The boys saw the word cinema and thought they'd like to go inside. Back then, there were no ratings certificates, so kids could watch anything in theory.

The doorman smiled at them and Chris and said "children welcome". (!)

~

Chris arrived at the studio with two crying boys complaining that their mum was so mean she wouldn't even let them go the cinema.

It wasn't until someone put me right that I discovered "Linda" was in fact a bloke. He was a full-on transvestite, that is, and he certainly had me fooled. Perhaps I should have guessed from the pearl earrings and necklaces Linda's dogs used to wear!

Our local watering hole was a pub called The Ship, which sat next door to us on Wardour Street. The pair who ran it were another couple of larger-than-life characters. The landlord was a tall, rake thin guy called Sid but it was his wife—a big, blowsy, and extremely busty woman called Lila—who really ran the place. She always used to have her hair up in a huge, hairstyle, a bit like Elsie Tanner in Coronation Street. The only time I saw it looking out of place was one night when a few of us were in there drinking after work. All of a sudden we heard a loud crash and a lot of hollering.

We looked behind the bar to see Lila climbing to her feet with her hair all over the place and her ample bosom barely covered up. The potman had called and forgotten to shut the trapdoor that linked the cellar to the bar. Lila had stepped back and fallen straight down the hole. It was a scene straight out of Only Fools And Horses, when Del Boy leant on the non-existent bar and fell flat on his face. Outwardly everyone in the pub expressed their concern, but inwardly we were all crying with laughter.

All sorts of people used to hang out in The Ship, musicians and entertainers alike. Tommy Cooper was a regular, as his agent's office was around the corner. Anyone with any sense left Tommy to himself when he was drinking. It was always the best policy with comics off duty—especially Tommy.

One day a session player who'd been working at the studio made the mistake of going up to Tommy at lunchtime in The Ship. Worse still, after telling him how pleased he was to meet him he asked him to tell a joke.

Everyone took a sharp intake of breath the minute he said it. We all knew Tommy had a bit of a temper on him. For a second I thought Tommy would stick one on him. But he didn't.

Instead Tommy leant back and gave him a look.

"And what do you do for a living son?" he asked.

"I play the trumpet sir," he said, pulling a deferential face.

"Well," said Tommy, "Play us a fucking tune then."

We all shifted around in our chairs suppressing our laughter as the poor lad turned purple with embarrassment.

Everywhere you turned there were mad characters. Most days walking down Wardour Street I'd notice a character called Old Rose, who used to run around with a carnation stuck behind his ear and had found a few moments of fame when he featured on the cover of The Beatles' Sgt. Pepper's Lonely Hearts Club Band. And then there was another silly old sod who walked around with a plastic tap stuck on his head because he had "water on the brain". There were artists, chancers, and even gangsters hanging around in the late night drinking dens. All human life was there—and then some . . .

And yet, as the sixties drew to a close and Trident got into its stride, Soho's cast of curious characters were soon looking quite dull compared to the legion of oddballs, eccentrics, and geniuses that began passing through our doors.

Three

Lord Of The Ringlets

"
Mr. Sheffield, we thought you should see this,
he said, handing me one of our own seven inch tape boxes
with the Trident label on it
"

One lunchtime, in April, a month after Trident had opened for business, I saw a couple of musicians walking in through reception carrying their instruments and heading down to the studio. These were very early days for us, so the arrival of new artists was still a novelty. This pair both looked like pretty typical products of the Summer of 1968, the era of "flower power." Both had a mass of long, curly hair and looked like they could do with a good wash. It was the smaller of the two who really caught my eye. There was something about him. He walked in looking like a little boy lost, carrying a large, heavily thumbed book under his arm. It turned out to be a copy of The Hobbit.

Thinking back on it, he could have been a character from a Tolkien book. He could have been the Lord of The Ringlets.

I checked with the receptionist and saw that the firm responsible for booking the odd pair was a group called Essex Music. The kid with the Tolkien under his arm was called Marc Bolan. It turned out the other guy was a bongo player called Steve Peregrine Took; together they were called Tyrannosaurus Rex.

A bright and enthusiastic New Yorker named Tony Visconti brought them over to us. Visconti was a funny character himself, and he happily admitted that he'd come over to London in order to "steal all the secrets" of the British record producer trade. Tony was working for Denny Cordell at Essex Music, based over on Oxford Street, and had been impressed by Tyrannosaurus Rex when he'd seen them playing live at a folk club.

Like a lot of sixties bands, Tyrannosaurus Rex were a band looking for a hit. Marc Bolan—who was actually born Mark Feld and had used a variety of other stage names—had released a single called "The Wizard" a year or two back which had nearly done the trick. For a while Simon Napier Bell had managed him, sticking the chap in an arty band called John's Children. Marc had managed to get himself noticed there by getting banned by the BBC. He'd written a song called "Desdemona", which the Beeb had objected to on the grounds that it had a line that went "lift up your skirt and fly". Pretty tame stuff by today's standards, but it was nothing short of heresy back then.

John's Children had fallen apart pretty quickly, and Bolan hooked up with his bongo-paying pal Peregrine Took and formed Tyrannosaurus Rex. They were very folky and far out. Their songs were very influenced by The Lord of the Rings and all that stuff. They'd played at that summer's Hyde Park festival with a few bands, among them another psychedelic band called The Pink Floyd. By all accounts, the show had gone down well.

They'd already recorded an album over at the Advision Studios. It hadn't even been released yet, but there was a bit of a buzz about the band. John Peel at BBC Radio 1 was championing them, and Tony Visconti had heard something he liked too.

Tony thought Marc had newer and better material than the stuff on his album and wanted to get it recorded fast. What we didn't know was that he'd booked time with us without his company's permission. Tony had hoped they'd be pleased at his initiative. As it turned out they were flabbergasted at his nerve!

By now word was spreading about our abilities. After Manfred Mann, we'd recorded with Alan Price, the keyboard player from The Animals. His single "Simon Smith and the Amazing Dancing Bear" had been a big hit too.

Through connections we'd made at our old studio, we'd also recorded The Small Faces' album Ogdens' Nut Gone Flake. We'd been really pleased with the work we'd done on that, and were even more proud when the record shot to number one on the album charts, another valuable first for us that did us no end of good within the industry. The Small Faces' album had quite a psychedelic feel to it, which was one of the reasons Tony Visconti had thought of us for Tyrannosaurus Rex.

Tony wanted to develop the Tyrannosaurus Rex sound. In particular he wanted to work on a song called "Debora", which another studio had been working on. It was a bit of a tall order, truth be told. Marc and his sidekick Took were penniless musicians. Apparently the demise of John's Children had been sped up by the fact that they'd had most of their gear nicked. Between them, all Tyrannosaurus Rex had was Marc's twelve quid guitar, a set of bongos, and a collection of odd and exotic instruments that you wouldn't normally find in any recording studio, let alone a brand new state of the art set up.

Tony's idea was that our technology would maximise the sound you got out of the limited resources they had by adding lots of reverb, overdubbing, and other effects.

We gave Malcolm Toft the job of working with them. It's fair to say he wasn't taken by their mixture of "out there" folk and psychedelic rock. He found it strange the way that Marc and Took would play nose flutes, tabla drums, Indian kazoos, and goodness knows what. He kept moaning to me and Barry that he wished Marc would do a bit of rock 'n' roll. He could see the potential he had; he just didn't like the approach they were taking.

But whenever he even hinted at this by saying "It would be nice to drop a bit of electric guitar in here," Marc would shake his head and say, "Oh, no we don't have the amplifiers or stuff like that."

The fact that Marc and Tony wanted to do complicated overdubbing, even though Marc only had two instruments, predictably caused problems from the outset and it soon caused friction in the studio.

My aim at the time was to make sure everyone enjoyed working at Trident. Whether it was our receptionist Penny or the biggest recording star in the world, I wanted people to be happy. Maintaining a good atmosphere was top of my list of priorities. So when I picked up on the fact that Malcolm didn't like what Tyrannosaurus Rex were up to, I thought I'd take the heat out of the situation by making a joke of it. I'd stick my head in the studio and if Malcolm was alone fiddling with Bolan's latest song, I'd take the mickey out of him and say, "Old Tofty, doing that T. Rex stuff again." I'm not sure it worked. I think he felt we were laughing at him rather than with him, I think.

It's not the end of the world if an engineer dislikes an artist's style, of course. There had been plenty who'd despised working with particular musicians. But it was preferable if there was some empathy there. And it was definitely preferable that the artist didn't know the engineer disliked his work. Unfortunately, in this case that wasn't possible.

Within a day or so Marc and Tony had picked up on Malcolm's attitude towards what they were doing. They were ready to walk out of the sessions because Malcolm wasn't giving them what they wanted. At one point, Marc and Tony had quite an animated discussion along those lines. If things had worked out differently, they'd have packed up their instruments—sparse as they were—and gone before we'd have known what had happened. Fortunately, Malcolm overheard their conversation and approached them. To his credit, he was straight with them.

"Tony, I honestly admit I don't like the band and don't understand the music," he said. All looked lost, but then he suggested a radical—but rather elegant—solution. "But I notice that you understand engineering and I bet if I coached you a little bit you could take over the recording." Tony agreed, and things were soon back on track.

It was a bold move, and not necessarily one I'd have backed if I'd known about it in advance. It wasn't the way things were done—or the way they had been done until now, at least. Certainly, if Malcolm had done that at CBS he'd have been sacked on the spot. But it did kind of typify the spirit we wanted to produce at Trident. We wanted it to be a freewheeling, anything goes place; well, to a point. One day during his time with us, Marc and his freewheeling lifestyle almost landed me in the shit, big time.

Early that morning the tea boy came into my office with the post.

"Mr. Sheffield, we thought you should see this," he said, handing me one of our own seven inch tape boxes with the Trident label on it.

It was addressed to Marc Bolan at an address in Cornwall.

The tape box had been opened by the Post Office and put in a new outer envelope with the words "Marked return to sender, gone away." I opened the box and knew what was in it immediately. It was absolutely full to the brim with hash. It must have been worth a small fortune.

I was horrified. All sorts of thoughts began to rush through my head. Despite the more liberal approach many artists took to drug use at the time, it was still illegal—and it was my responsibility to ensure it didn't happen on the property. I had known this from the outset and made it clear to anyone who worked at the studio that this was the rule. No ifs, no buts. Or should that be butts? Anyhow, my first thought was that someone was setting us up. The Post Office had clearly identified the substance inside the box was and sent it back to me. I had an awful feeling in my gut that we were going to get a "visit" at any moment.

I dashed down to the studio, where I found my brother in the control room. I called him outside and showed him the box. Barry was as shocked as me.

"I think I should take it straight to the police," I said.

He nodded in agreement.

So I headed straight out the door and headed for our nearest police station, Savile Row, about half a mile away. I knew one or two of the coppers there and, if there was any trouble, hoped they might put in a good word for me.

As usual, the streets of Soho were filled with colourful characters. I couldn't help laughing at the irony. This stuff was like gold dust around here. I'd have been the most popular man in London if they'd known what was inside the box.

When I got to Savile Row there was a long queue at the desk. I was too agitated to hang around so just marched up and asked for a CID.

"Go to the back of the queue and wait your turn like everyone else sir," the duty Sergeant said, unimpressed by my pushiness.

Instead I stepped to the side of the counter, which didn't go down well. "Go to the back of the queue sir," he repeated.

By now I'd taken the box out of the envelope. I put it on the top of the reception desk, shoved it in his direction then lifted the edge of it open so that he could see inside.

I thought his eyes were going to jump out of his head. They were on stalks. He looked at me as if I must have been stark, staring mad. "What sort of idiot brings that into a police station," he must have been saying to himself.

Within ten seconds I had two CID officers inviting me into their office.

I wasn't sure they'd buy my explanation. I'm not sure I'd have bought it myself, to be honest. It did sound dodgy.

But they accepted it and eventually thanked me for bringing in the box. They assured me they'd destroy its contents, which made me laugh. There were several ways of doing that, some of which were more pleasurable than others.

I walked back through Soho feeling a mixture of relief and hilarity. How the hell had I got away with that one?

I had a stiff drink before heading back into the office. I could hear Tony Visconti and Malcolm Toft working away on some Tyrannosaurus Rex stuff, but decided against telling them about it. I didn't mention it to Marc either. I didn't see the point.

Once Malcolm, Marc, and Tony had cleared the air, things improved enormously in the studio. Tony took to sound engineering like a duck to water. Under Malcolm's watchful eye, he was soon evolving Tyrannosaurus Rex's sound. He also got quite ambitious. The most notable track on the album, which came to be known as Prophets, Seers & Sages: The Angels of the Ages, was a song called "Deboraarobed". It was exactly what it sounded like, a song which played backwards in the second half. It was innovative, if nothing else. There was a good atmosphere in the studio as well. John Peel turned up one day to play tambourine during one of the sessions. After their shaky start, Malcolm and Tony got on like a house on fire. Tony was into astrology, and when he found out that Malcolm was the same star sign as him things got even better.

It wouldn't be long before Marc Bolan made it. That was obvious. There was something about him, a quality that I only saw a few times during my years at Trident. His breakthrough came a couple of years later, in 1970. By that time he'd sacked his mate Peregrine Took from the band—now rechristened T. Rex—hooked up with another percussionist named Mickey Finn, bought himself a Les Paul electric guitar, and followed Malcolm Toft's advice.

Around that time a new engineer had joined the Trident team as well, a chap named Roy Baker. We all knew him as RTB, however, since his full name was Roy Thomas Baker. Was assigned him the T. Rex project with Tony.

Together with Marc they soon produced T. Rex's breakthrough single, "Ride a White Swan". The song was credited with launching a new pop movement known as "glam rock". For the next couple of years, hits like "Get It On", "Jeepster", and "Metal Guru" kept Marc at the top of the charts, and made him a rock 'n' roll star.

No one had done more to help Marc during his early days than Malcolm Toft. Knowing that Marc didn't have two pennies to rub together, Malcolm even used to give Marc a lift home late at night after recording sessions.

So he was disappointed—if not altogether surprised—when he met Marc on Wardour Street at the height of his fame a few years later. "He didn't really want to know me. He was telling me about his Rolls Royce, his big house, and this and that. He was very arrogant," Malcolm later told me.

It was a pattern we'd see repeated far too often. Fame, money, and success can have a strange and sometimes destructive effect on people.

~

That wasn't something you could say about The Beatles, certainly not as individuals. I always found them great to work with, real professionals. But there was no question that by 1968 their new venture, known as Apple, was running a bit out of control.

Apple Records had been one of the first companies to approach us when we'd opened up the studio. I'd had a good relationship with Peter Asher, who ran their A&R. As a result they sent a lot of their artists to us.

The Beatles had this thing about literally giving anybody an audition. So they wasted a lot of studio time booking in acts just so they could see what they sounded like. The people they sent our way were a really odd collection of individuals.

One guy who turned up for a session was totally off his head. Malcolm Toft was in the studio when this guy started singing. He couldn't believe his ears.

He kept singing the same words over and over again. Or to be precise he kept singing "Around and around and around . . ." Ad bloody nauseam. And it wasn't even in tempo.

Of course, not everything they sent us was rubbish. In the summer of 1968 they brought a young Welsh singer named Mary Hopkin over to us. She recorded the ballad "Those Were the Days" at the studio, which Paul McCartney produced. It was a mega hit. Afterwards Apple sent us a lot more work—including James Taylor, Badfinger, Billy Preston, Doris Troy, Ravi Shankar, Jackie Lomax, Ronnie Specter, and of course the Fab Four themselves for their eventful recording of "Hey Jude".

~

"Hey Jude" came out on Friday, August 30th, 1968. It really did mark Trident's arrival on the music scene in London. The phone was ringing red-hot in the days and weeks afterwards. People wanted to know more about us and what we could do for their artists.

As far as The Beatles were concerned, however, they already knew the answer to that question. Even before the release of "Hey Jude", they'd been back in the studio with us recording tracks for their new self-titled album, which became known to most people as the White Album.

They'd first arrived on the Wednesday before "Hey Jude" came out. There was no doubt in my mind that they'd been blown away by the possibilities our 8-track opened up for them. That day they began a marathon fourteen-hour session that ran from five in the afternoon to seven the following morning. During that particular session they'd managed to hammer out a new song by John, "Dear Prudence".

From a financial point of view it was amazing. They may have done so through gritted teeth, but EMI underwrote everything The Beatles did without question. They wrote us a cheque for the studio hire, blank tape, and engineers' overtime they'd run up during that session. And the band was back for more of the same the next two nights.

It may well have been that rumblings at EMI about the cost of our studio got back to them. The company was not used to paying third party studio bills, and did not suffer it lightly.

I heard that the following week The Beatles "liberated" the 8-track machine EMI had been testing endlessly at Abbey Road. Somehow they'd moved it from a technician's office into Studio 2, almost getting an engineer named Dave Harries sacked for his collaboration.

It wasn't long before the boys were back, however. During the first week of October they spent another five days with us, recording Paul's songs "Honey Pie" and "Martha My Dear", as well as another song of George's (apparently inspired by their session guitarist Eric Clapton's love of chocolate!) called "Savoy Truffle". We also recorded "I Want You (She's So Heavy)" which was used on "Abbey Road"

A lot of rumours were flying around about trouble in the band at the time. George Martin wasn't around as much as he used to be, and Ringo—apparently—quit the band halfway through August, for a few days at least. But there was no real sign of that when they were with us. The atmosphere in the studio when The Beatles were in was fabulous. Everyone worked hard, but they had fun too. Sometimes a little bit too much.

One day it was someone's birthday. It may well have been their ubiquitous right hand man Mal Evans. George Harrison arrived with a birthday cake, which he promptly brought into the control room.

"Here we go lads," he said. "Enough for everyone."

We were very strict on not allowing food in there. We couldn't risk it. The control room and the mixing desk was no place to be eating Chinese takeaways. We had a kitchen upstairs where people could go and make food and eat it. Cake was another matter, however. In the studio with us that day was one of our regular session musicians, an old mate of mine who'd helped me with the construction of the studio, Jerry Salisbury. "Go on Jerry, run upstairs, cut the cake up, and make a pot of tea," someone said.

He happily obliged.

Jerry arrived back down about ten or fifteen minutes later. As he was climbing the small step that led back into the control room he tripped and went flying, almost pouring the tea all over me, Barry, and The Beatles. Everyone fell about laughing

It was only a little later that we worked out what had happened. It turned out George's cake was one of his "special cakes". It was full of hash.

Barry and I didn't really notice it. But Jerry did. He'd helped himself to a large corner of the cake when he'd been upstairs making the tea. It had obviously had an immediate impact on him. He was off his face.

Another memorable moment came one evening Gerry came to my office.

"There are some gentlemen here to see you," he said ominously.

My face must have drained when I saw who was standing, waiting for me by the entrance. It was a senior policeman, his helmet covered in all the silver spaghetti that comes with a high rank.

"Oh shit," I thought to myself. "This could be trouble."

Virtually every studio had gone through a spell of going through drug busts, but we had avoided it somehow. I knew the boys liked a smoke, but I had no idea what they had on them. John and George were my biggest worry. Suddenly I had visions of the cops marching them out of Trident—and taking our future with them.

Fortunately, he wasn't there to conduct a raid. The copper was a really chatty guy and just asked me what was going on. The crowds were still outside, so he knew full well who was inside the studio. I offered him a drink in my office, which he accepted. He hung around for a while, I think hoping to get a glimpse of the boys.

The place was thick with the smell of Joss sticks mingling with other perfumes and eventually by agreement with the boys he was allowed into the control room. You could have cut the atmosphere with a knife, but all he really wanted was a set of autographs.

He left a very happy man. I poured myself a very large drink when he left.

~

Aside from recording their own stuff, The Beatles continued to send Apple artists in to us by the bushel.

The first non-British artist they'd signed up was the American folk singer James Taylor. Around the same time as they were making The White Album, Taylor recorded his first album with us, with Paul McCartney playing bass on a couple of tracks.

McCartney actually produced parts of it as well, with Barry sitting in as engineer. Paul, like John, George, and even Ringo, was professional to the core. He just wanted to come into the studio and do the best possible job he could, and he respected the pros around him. Tofty was chuffed to bits when, during one session together, Paul poured him a glass of beer. He still considers that an honour.

That winter of 1968 and the following spring of 1969 was a huge turning point for The Beatles. Apple became even more chaotic, leading to Peter Asher's departure and the arrival of a new manager for the band in the shape of a tough American lawyer called Alan Klein. But huge rifts were also opening up between John and Paul. It was clear things were changing. I got a personal glimpse into that a couple of months after The White Album.

My heart had actually sunk a little bit when, one day in the spring of 1969, I heard the voice of John Lennon on the other end of the line. I knew exactly why he was calling me.

"Hi Norman. What have you got?" he said, cutting to the chase.

I decided to be honest.

"Well, I've got it all, but I haven't got a bloody clue where I'm going with it John," I said.

There were times when John would have laughed out loud at that. But that day wasn't one of them.

"Hold on, I'll come round and I'll walk you through it," he said.

It was March, 1969, and a few days earlier John, Yoko, and a group of other musicians had taken to a stage in Cambridge to perform a new, improvised piece of music, called "Unfinished Music No. 2: Life with the Lions".

As the name suggested, it was the second piece like this that they'd done. The first one had been called "Unfinished Music No. 1: Two Virgins", and had been really controversial.

John asked Barry and me to go to Cambridge and record the "Life with the Lions" project live. He had also asked whether we could record it on video, as we had one of the first Sony reel-to-reel video tape recorders and cameras.

This was a real blind project for us, and as the show unfolded it became even more confusing. God knows what the audience thought of it. The piece was a mixture of Yoko's vocals, electric guitar feedback from John, some stuff from sax player John Tchicai, and percussion from John Stevens towards the end of the piece. The music was almost entirely continuous. There were no tracks per se, so all we could do was to record and shoot continuously, waiting for someone to stop and take a breath so that we could change the reels.

We then took the tapes back to Trident. We couldn't make head or tail of them either, as we had been unable to make notes or markings. It was weird, very experimental stuff. As far as we could make out, there were some Japanese people and some English people on there. But it was a real hodgepodge. It was the strangest thing I'd ever been involved in.

John was as good as his word and arrived later that day. John was always very professional. He rolled up his sleeves and got down to work. We did two or three days work on it.

It was clear he was doing it for her. He and Yoko were joined at the hip. Literally. I'd seen some of it during the recording of The White Album the previous year. He was determined to make t his work.

John was very focused when he was in the studio, as all The Beatles were. He smoked, but he didn't drink. He got the job done. But he was also a good laugh. He was a character.

One day he was down in the studio, adding something to this piece. There were two big monitors in the corner, mounted high on the back wall, where some chairs were stacked. John suddenly climbed on the top of the chairs, wobbling around like some stilt walker.

"Just play it back through here," he said, sticking his head up to these monitors. We all had a laugh at that, although deep down a little part of me was panicking that he'd fall and break his bloody neck. I didn't want Trident to go down in history as the place where one of The Beatles crippled himself.

He clearly grew to trust me—and the rest of the guys at Trident. One day not long after we'd finished straightening out Yoko's piece, I got a message from Apple to ring John Lennon.

"Norman, can you come round here and have a look at these monitors we've bought for the boardroom?" he said when I got through to him.

"Sure," I said.

I went round to Apple in Savile Row and met John there. It turned out they'd bought a hi-fi system and had forked out god knows how much for it. It really wasn't much good at all, and it had been fitted in incorrectly. It all needed lining up.

"I play my stuff into it and it sounds awful," John said to me. "What do I do?"

I just looked at him and said, "Take it out and start again."

He just shook his head. I could see what he was thinking. He thought he was surrounded by amateurs, which at that point in Apple's history he probably was.

"Do it, will you? Spend what you need to spend."

So we ended up rewiring parts of the Apple building so that they had decent sound equipment.

It wasn't long after that the end came. I wasn't that surprised to be honest. Paul announced that he was leaving the band and the whole thing turned kind of nasty. For a long time there was a lot of bad feeling between them all.

We continued to work with them individually. George Harrison in particular was a regular. But there was a real feeling that The Beatles era had come to an end. It was time for a new guard to take over.

Four

Sitting In A Tin Can

"Space Oddity" in many ways summed up that early Trident ethos

By the end of our first nine months in business at Trident we had had four top ten singles. Success breeds success, so by late 1969 we were getting some of the music industry's brightest young talents in through the doors. That autumn and winter, bands like Procol Harum, Amen Corner, Fairport Convention, and Blind Faith—the so-called "supergroup" formed by Eric Clapton, Steve Winwood, and Ginger Baker—all recorded with us.

Despite the troubles that the company was going through, Apple continued to feed us work with artists like Jackie Lomax, Marsha Hunt, and the Modern Jazz Quartet taking turns in the studio.

We had a couple of things going for us that were setting us apart from the competition. By now we'd upgraded our equipment so to accommodate 16-track recording, again the first in London. We'd also led the way in the UK by introducing, in January that year, the first Dolby noise reduction system. A lot of people were coming over just out of curiosity to see what our equipment could do. Nowhere else had this stuff, not even EMI at Abbey Road.

But our popularity came mostly due to the aura that was building around the place, the idea that we were a young, "happening" place. The era of the laboratory recording studios really was coming to an end. People wanted to be surrounded by young, creative people. They wanted to bounce things off each other. We were always happy to accommodate this. We were in the right place in Soho, and we had the talent to bring out an artist's creativity.

By now we'd taken on more engineering staff. That year we'd acquired a new engineer by the name of Ken Scott. Ken had worked with The Beatles at EMI, but he'd fallen out with them during the making of The White Album.

The new manager at the studio, Alan Stagge, had even fired Ken at one point, so Ken went to the head of EMI and has the decision overturned. But even though he'd won the battle, Ken knew he'd lose the war.

So he'd asked another successful producer, Gus Dudgeon, for some advice. Gus had recommended he talk to Barry and me. We'd taken him on like a shot and began educating him in the Trident way, which was very different to what he'd been used to at EMI. He found it incredibly liberating.

The other thing we had going for us was a reputation for going that extra mile to make things work for people—no matter what. The leader of the Modern Jazz Quartet, John Lewis, had been so excited about working on our 8-track equipment that he rewrote part of the album Space for two pianos. He asked us whether we could find a Steinway piano that was a close match to the Trident Bechstein. I personally helped John find it—and the results were magical.

On another occasion, a client wanted an eight foot long Marimba. A local percussion specialist in Archer Street about a quarter of a mile away named Doc Hunt had one, but he couldn't deliver it or break it down. So Gerry Salisbury took one of the tea boys with him and decided to push this giant instrument in its full, playable state all the way up the middle of Wardour Street. It clogged up the Soho traffic for half an hour, much to the displeasure of the cabbies, who let Gerry know exactly what they thought of him. But he didn't care—we delivered what the client wanted.

~

To be honest, we'd taken off faster than we—or anyone else—had imagined. Our deal with Dunbar Securities meant that we'd regain a controlling interest in the studio when we recorded our first annual profit of £50,000. They'd guessed that it would take us five years to do that. We thought that was pretty realistic too. But we'd surprised them—and ourselves—and done it within the first year. We were determined to reinvest the money we were making and to keep doing what we were doing—staying ahead of the game and creating a new recording environment unlike anything else in London, or anywhere else for that matter.

To that end, in November 1968 I'd started visiting the US. Michael Jardine -Patterson accompanied me the first time when I went to visit Ampex Recorders, mainly to sort the problems that we had with our original 8-track machine motors. I also wanted to see what was in development so that we remained one step ahead.

Our timing was great. We had been the first studio to buy an Ampex 8-track outside of the USA and the impact was immediate. Our recordings of "Hey Jude" and "Those Were The Days" were numbers one and two, respectively, on the Billboard charts. So I felt like I was in a strong position to tell them what I thought about their equipment.

We arrived at the Ampex offices in Redwood City, now part of Silicon Valley, to meet with the CEO, Al Saroka. He was a big guy, and as we sat in his office he removed his jacket to reveal he was wearing a gun. My ideas of giving him a rollicking quickly faded.

To be fair he was extremely helpful and apologetic. When he asked me what spares we needed I rang back to London and spoke to Ron Goodwin our head of maintenance and asked him what he wanted?

"Scrounge everything," he said.

I almost brought back a complete 8-track machine as hand luggage.

~

Life at Trident was never dull. The acts that came through our doors made sure of that.

The sixties were a crazy time. It seemed like the crazier you were the more chance you had of succeeding. No one was crazier than Viv Stanshall, the leader of the Bonzo Dog Doo Dah Band, who recorded with us in that year.

They were big favourites of Paul McCartney, who with Gus Dudgeon and under the pseudonym of "Apollo C. Vermouth" had produced their surprise chart hit, "I'm the Urban Spaceman". They'd come to us to record more wacky material, including their albums The Doughnut In Granny's Greenhouse and Tadpoles, both of which were produced by

Gus Dudgeon and engineered by Barry. The last album they recorded with us was called Keysham, which featured Gerry Salisbury, our multi-tasking Jack of All Trades, on jazz cornet during the song "Busted." The album notes credited him with "jazz cornet and fish 'n chips".

Viv was the undoubted leader of the band and was a sixteen-carat crackpot. I couldn't work with him. He was just too bonkers. He'd have me in stitches with the things he did. Barry was the same. When Viv was in, Barry would be crying with laughter all day long.

With Viv you simply never knew what was going to happen.

One day I was in the office upstairs and my brother rang me.

"Norman, come down, you've got to see this," he said. I could hear hysterical laughter in the background.

I walked into the control room and looked down into the studio. For a moment or two I couldn't work out what the hell I was looking at, but I eventually it started to come together.

There was a mannequin mounted on roller-skates that was—somehow—being remotely controlled by a member of the band, I think it was Neil Innes. It had no clothes on and was dashing around the studio—blowing bubbles out of its backside.

Despite his anarchic behaviour, however, Viv was always a gent. I heard a great story about him when, later that year, they did a really successful tour of America. (What the hell they made of the Bonzos over there I have no idea.) Anyhow, one day Viv and the band were pulled over by a traffic policeman. He asked them if they had any firearms on them, to which they replied "no". The cop looked perplexed. "So how are you going to defend yourselves then?" he asked the band. Viv stepped forward and smiled at him. "With good manners," he said.

That was the thing about Trident. People came along and behaved creatively and sometimes a little crazily, but they respected the place and what we were doing. Well, most of them did, at least.

～

Of course, you'd get the odd idiot, who thought they knew everything. I remember when an American producer and singer, Terry Melcher, the son of Doris Day, came over to record. He'd worked with all sorts of artists in the States, including The Byrds, Glen Campbell, and The Mamas and the Papas, and was even friendly with Brian Wilson of the Beach Boys.

He had a lot of recording experience, but his attitude from the beginning was that British recording studios were rubbish in comparison to American ones. At the end of the session, he got up and said to Barry, "Okay, it wasn't that bad, but I've known better." He then gave Barry a fiver and said in a really condescending voice, "Get yourself a drink."

Barry did exactly what I'd have done.

He turned to this pillock and said, "To be honest with you Terry, you can ram it up your backside. I don't need your money, I own this place."

He never came back to Trident, needless to say. We found out later that, while he was working with us at the studio, the Charles Manson clan took over his old house in Beverly Hills, murdering Sharon Tate and several of her friends. Rumour had it that Manson had been after Terry!

~

Recording at Trident was always an unpredictable affair. And we were always learning new tricks. Marc Bolan and his newly rechristened band T. Rex still came by on occasion to record with us. Even though he became pretty arrogant, Marc had a genuine affection for Trident where, after all, he'd cut his teeth with Tony Visconti.

To get a natural reverb sound, we'd often use the men's toilets to record bits and pieces. It was a tiled room just off the studio, and it gave us the perfect, almost metallic sound we wanted.

One day we needed some hand clapping on a T-Rex song. It had become something of a signature-sound for them. When recorded it in the studio it sounded a bit dead. Tony knew the studio well and knew that we occasionally used the toilet.

Marc gave Tony a funny look when he said, "Let's go in the men's room and clap our hands there."

We rigged up a mike in there and gave it a whirl. It worked a treat.

In fact it worked so well, we put some saxophones and guitar amps in there and began recording a whole load of stuff.

Marc thought it was hilarious—but he could also hear that it worked.

The only people who weren't happy about it were the merchants down below us in St. Anne's Court. They could hear all this stuff going on through the ventilation grating.

Before we knew it we had a sandwich maker and a watch repairer banging on our front door complaining. If only they'd known they were hearing rock 'n' roll history!

~

Another reason for our growing success, I think, was the fact that producers and record companies trusted us. They didn't think we were out to rip them off and rack up as much recording time as possible when their artists came to record with us. In fact, there were times when it was quite the opposite. We took a great deal of trouble choosing which engineer would suit each artist, producer best, this would usually result in a long relationship with artists returning to us many times over the coming years.

Around that time, Joe Cocker came in to record his album With A Little Help From My Friends.

The producer was a guy called Denny Cordell. He was very good, but he was pedantic. Very pedantic. He'd used four different studios and had even sent the horn part of the song to America to be worked on.

They were trying to record "Bye, Bye Blackbird" with us. It was going on and on and on. It wasn't for us to interfere in the process. We could make suggestions, but ultimately it was down to the artist and the producer.

One night I got a call from David Platt, the head of the label.

"For Christ's sake Norman, can you do something to get them out of there? Even if this bloody album goes double platinum I won't make a profit," he said.

"Let me see what I can do," I said.

I went down to the control room to see what was going on. They were still tinkering with it. When Denny went down into the studio to have a word with the musicians, I took the opportunity and had a word with Tony Visconti, who was working as the mixing engineer.

"Look Tony, we've got to persuade him that this is finished," I said.

So together we approached Denny when he came back. We made up some cock and bull story about us needing to do some maintenance in the studio and suggested we all come back the next day.

"Sounds like you're nearly there anyhow," I said to him, hoping that might help him get a decent night's sleep and come back refreshed. Sometimes, all an artist needs is a break. When Denny came back the following day he nailed it within an hour.

I got a phone call from David Platt thanking me not long afterwards. And, of course, he sent me a lot more business too.

There was a sense that we were part of a large, extended family. Like all families, we had our black sheep and our favourite aunties and uncles. But we were family and we stuck together.

That feeling was underlined when Tony Visconti worked with Mary Hopkin on her second album.

During the recording it was pretty clear to a lot of us that there was more than just a creative spark between Tony and Mary. Sure enough they got married in 1971, and had a couple of lovely children together.

I like to think we fired Cupid's arrow there, or maybe it was Cupid's trident.

~

Compared to some of the loons that came through our door, the young singer-songwriter David Bowie was a model of common sense. He was a mate of Marc Bolan and had been trying to break through for a few years. Tony Visconti had heard his first album and had been intrigued, even though he thought it was "all over the place, style-wise." He'd met and started talking to Bowie and really liked him. Bowie was essentially a nice guy. He was young, bright, and trying to learn his trade. He had a lot of confidence but he was also open to lots of ideas and wasn't stuck on one type of music. He'd already been through a folky phase and a quirky phase in which he'd sounded like Anthony Newley on songs like "The Laughing Gnome". With Tony he was ready to move into a different kind of sound, with what Tony called a "twelve-string guitar, folk-rock feel."

They mapped out a plan for an album and Tony put together a band that he felt could bring it to life. But as they started work in the summer of 1969 they hit a problem.

David had written a song called "Space Oddity", a number about a bloke going off into outer space. The world was obsessed with the Apollo mission at the time. We were within a month of man walking on the moon. Tony thought the song and lines like "here am I sitting in a tin can" was a "cheap shot" and "just a jingle for the moon shot." He also thought the middle eight sounded too much like Simon & Garfunkel's "Bookends" and that David was singing like John Lennon.

He was, as he admits himself, "very idealistic and very inflexible" at the time, and told David what he thought. He said that "Space Oddity" didn't fit with the person he'd got to know, who was more thoughtful and original than that. "It's not you," he told David, adding that he wasn't going to record it, partly because he simply didn't have the experience to "come up with the science fiction-type backing that would be required."

The problem was that Bowie had already played the song to Mercury Records, who really liked it. He was kind of obliged to record.

All this left Tony Visconti in a bit of a bad situation. The Trident philosophy came to his rescue. Tony had benefited from our free-flowing approach himself, of course, when Malcolm Toft had offered to teach him sound engineering during the Tyrannosaurus Rex sessions. Perhaps influenced by the memory of that, he suggested to Bowie that he talk to Gus Dudgeon, who had been "waxing lyrical" about his work. Gus agreed to produce the single "Space Oddity" with Barry engineering. They went into the studio to record on Saturday

June 20th, 1969.Tony Visconti came back later and recorded the Space oddity album with Ken Scott engineering.

The session didn't take long at all. It was laid down in three hours. Rick Wakeman played Melotron and Mick Ronson was playing guitar and during the middle eight of the song, he did this solo, almost tongue-in-cheek. Afterwards ,Gus Dudgeon was going to make him do it again, but Barry thought he was wrong.

One of Barry's philosophies was that you either liked something or you didn't like something the first time you hear it. "There's not much music that grows on people," he always used to say.

The moment he heard the guitar he knew he liked it.

"You can't change that, Gus," he said. "Leave it in, it's a one-off, if you muck about with it, it'll go wrong."

Fortunately, Gus listened—and one of the most memorable bits of the record was saved. I still think of that whenever I hear the song, which is pretty often, even now, forty years later. I am sure it was the world's first stereo single.

~

"Space Oddity" in many ways summed up that early Trident ethos.

What was great was that after the recording was finished, Tony went to David and said that he assumed he'd now do the rest of the album with Gus Dudgeon.

But Bowie said, "No, I've got that out of the way now and I want to work with you." It was an amazing act of loyalty, not the sort of thing you'd expect in the rock 'n' roll industry, where there were more sharks than in the South China Sea.

The most memorable part of the recording of that album came when Bowie was recording "Wild Eyed Boy From Freecloud", which was also going to be the B-side of "Space Oddity".

It was one of the very first things we did with the new 16-track machine.

Visconti had a massive, fifty-strong orchestra booked, which immediately rang alarm bells for us. Ever since "Hey Jude" we'd had trouble with classical musicians. They didn't come cheap and they were always a bit sniffy. They also used to insist on a fifteen to twenty minute break. Tony Visconti was the one who first spotted it. The same thing would happen almost every time. The string players would sit there reading the Financial Times, the woodwind players would flick through something less challenging and the brass players would rush out to the "models" in the building next door. They'd come back in a quarter of an hour later, with red faces and big grins.

Anyhow, in anticipation of trouble Tony made Barry and I promise that the 16-track was set up and working properly before they arrived at ten in the morning. We assured him that it already was and that everything would be fine.

This huge orchestra showed up on time and after an hour or so rehearsal, with Bowie sitting in the middle of the studio surrounded by all these musicians, we went for it.

Malcolm Toft was at the engineering desk and said, "Right, let's do the first take." We set the machines rolling, David sang the song and we headed back upstairs to hear the playback. I could have died on the spot. Tony said that it sounded like "the music was coming from behind a chip fryer." He recalled later, "It was full of hisses and crackles and snaps and pops, with a little bit of music in the background."

Barry and Ron Goodwin began frantically making adjustments, trying to iron out the problem. They only had the orchestra booked until 1 p.m. At 12.55 we decided we had to go for it. "Let's put one down," Malcolm said.

The musicians were looking at us all with utter contempt. There was no way on earth they were going to give us any free time. And if we went into overtime they were eligible to get double the fees, that was the way it worked with the Musician's Union then.

So we did the one take. And by the time it was done we saw the musicians packing up their cases. They were off.

David and Tony looked at each other. Fortunately when they got back up to the control room it was a good take. There was still a bit of the "chip fryer" in there, but there was enough for them to work with. Thank God!

Bowie was a really down-to-earth character. There were no airs and graces, no diva behaviour. He wanted to learn. But he was also a social animal and he had a sense of humour.

One day, the tea boys, Howard, came down from the kitchen with a fresh brew of tea. David took one sip of his and pulled a terrible face. It was as if someone had put salt in his tea, or something.

"Oh, God, what did you put in there," he said. "It tastes of kippers." (He'd left the kettle descaler in the kettle.)

Well that was one nickname sorted out. He was Kipper from that day onwards.

David would come for a drink in The Ship at the end of a recording session. But by then we were also drinking at a place called La Chasse, on the first floor of number 100, Wardour Street. David of course would be become a major client at Trident, Ken Scott would eventually produce David and make some of the finest albums of the time, Hunkey Dory, Ziggy Startdust, Aladdin Sane, Pin Ups.

That was another slice of Soho eccentricity. It was a crumbling ruin of a place run by a guy called Jack Barrie, who also ran the Marquee club a few doors down the street. I had first met Jack when we were working together at Apollo Music's small management operation, I was working with my old friends John Barker and Unit Four Plus Two, Kenny Everett and other DJs from off shore Radio London and he was managing a new band The Herd with Peter Frampton, also in that team was Billy Gaff who would become Rod Stewart's manager. It was little more than a room, and it was packed with as few as thirty people in there. Sometimes it was so thick with smoke you couldn't see from one side to the other. It was a real magnet for the music industry's lunatic fringe.

One night, Viv Stanshall and another of the biggest nutters in town, Keith Moon, the drummer with the Who, turned up in Nazi uniforms. They'd be arrested these days for dressing like that. But back then everyone thought it was a hoot.

Jack was another "character", although you had to watch his roving eye. Our young tea-boy, come engineer, Kipper, began drinking there with us. He was a good-looking lad. Bless him, he spent the first few months of his time at La Chasse thinking he'd been allowed in because he worked at Trident. It was only one night when he saw Jack eyeing him up that the penny dropped. Many was the time that poor old Kip had to fend off Jack's "nefarious advances".

La Chasse might have been a dump, but it was actually a great place for networking. Among those I got to know through drinking there was an ex-journalist called Tony Stratton-Smith. Tony looked after bands like The Bonzos, The Nice and Van der Graaf Generator. The latter's already legendary roadies, a mad pair called Crackie and one-eyed Noj, were always in La Chasse, usually off their faces.

Tony hadn't been able to get his acts record deals, so he'd set up his own label, Charisma Records. He told me that the first thing he was going to do was an album with Van der Graaf Generator called The Least We Can Do Is Wave To Each Other. We hit it off and the band recorded it with us during two intense days in December 1969. As the sixties turned into the 1970s, Tony Straton-Smith would become one of our biggest—and best—customers.

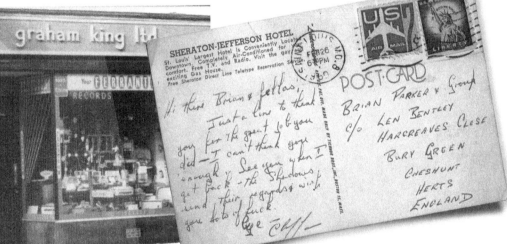

SHERATON-JEFFERSON HOTEL
St. Louis' Largest Hotel is Conveniently Located
Downtown. Completely Air-Conditioned for
comfort. Free T.V. and Radio. Visit the gay,
exciting Gas House.
Free Sheraton Direct Line Teletype Reservation Service

POST-CARD

Hi there Brian & fellas,
   Just a line to thank
you for the great job you
did — I can't thank you
enough! See you when I
get back — the Shadows
send their regards & wish
you lots of luck.
      Cliff

Brian Parker & Group
c/o Len Bentley
Hargreaves Close
Bury Green
Cheshunt
Herts
England

TEEN SCENE Fontana
The Hunters play The Big Hits

1960

1968

1968

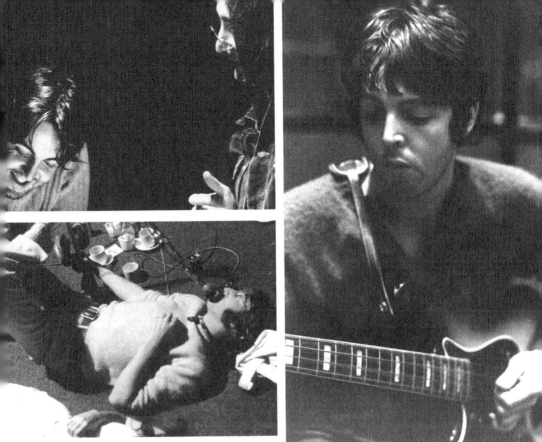

1970

1970

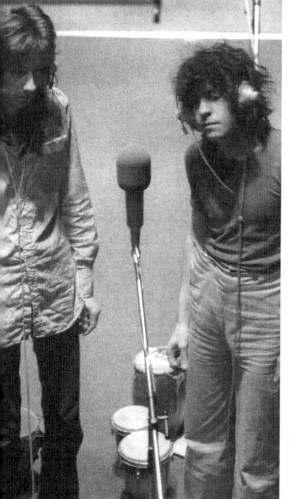

★ STAR-POWER ★
T.REX
Get It On

1960 (p.93-95) **FULL PAGE:** Norman playing behind Cliff Richard at Wembley Arena. **LEFT PAGE:** (clockwise) *Top:* Hazelwood youth club band. *Middle right:* Postcard from Cliff Richard to The Hunters. *Bottom right:* The Hunters about to leave for Wembley Arena and the Palladium. *Bottom left:* Dave Sampson and The Hunters publicity photograph. *Middle bottom left:* The Hunters first album "Teen Scene". *Middle left:* The Record Shop at Waltham Cross.
RIGHT PAGE: (clockwise) *Top:* The Hunters with Cliff Richard at Wembley Arena. *Middle right:* The Hunters on tour. *Bottom:* The Hunters Publicity photograph. *Middle left:* The Hunters line up.

1968 (p.96-97) **LEFT PAGE:** (clockwise) *Top left:* Norman and the team in St. Annes Court as it was in the 1960's. *Top right:* Norman and Barry discussing the works in progress. *Small middle right:* Building as it was purchased. *Middle right:* Top floor finally cleared. *Middle left:* Opening night – Norman,Robert iggulden,Barry, Michael Jardine-Patterson, Chris Sheffield, Sir David Hope-Dunbar. *Small right:* Air conditioning being installed in the studio. *Bottom:* Norman and Barry in the control room on opening night.
RIGHT PAGE: (clockwise) *Top Left:* Studio completed on March 8th 1968. Top right: Front of Trident House. *Lower top right:* The Ship Pub, Wardour Street. *Middle left:* Norman in his office. *Middle:* Manfred Mann "My Name's Jack" – Trident's first hit. *Middle right:* The original Trident tape machine room. *Bottom right:* The original remix room. *Bottom left:* Trident preview theatre.

1968 (p.98-99) **LEFT PAGE:** (clockwise) *Top Left:* The Beatles: John Lennon, Paul McCartney, a representative, Ringo Starr, George Harrison. Top right:

George Harrison in session. *Middle right:* Ringo Starr taking a moment on the Bechstein Grand Piano. Bottom: The Beatles "Hey Jude" sessions.
RIGHT PAGE: (clockwise) *Top left:* Paul and John sharing a story. *Top right:* Paul in session. *Bottom right:* John and Yoko Ono. *Bottom left:* John Lennon listening to playback. *Middle left:* The Beatles "Hey Jude" record sleve. *Middle left:* John Lennon taking a moment during a session.

1970 (p.100-101) **LEFT PAGE:** (clockwise) *Top:* In the control room at Trident with David Bowie Hermione Farthingale,Tony Visconti and John Hutchinson. *Bottom right:* Mick Ronson in action. *Bottom left:* David Bowie and Hermione Farthingale recording at Trident.
RIGHT PAGE: (clockwise) *Top left:* The Bonzo dog Doo Dah Band complete with mannequin! *Top right:* Joe Cocker. *Bottom right:* Ziggy Stardust Album Sleeve. *Bottom left:* David Bowie with John Hutchinson. *Middle left:* David Bowie with Mick Ronson.

1970 (p.102-103) **LEFT PAGE:** (clockwise) *Top left:* Elton John with Marc Bolan and Ringo Starr. *Middle right:* Roy Thomas Baker with Tony Visconti at work. *Bottom right:* T Rex 'Get it on' single sleeve. *Bottom left:* Mark Bolan with Steve Peregrin Took.
RIGHT PAGE: (clockwise) *Top:* Paul McCartney in the control room with Mary Hopkin 'listening to play back of 'Those Were The Days'. *Bottom:* Trident Studios playing cards depicting artists of the time.

Five

New Horizons

"Somehow one of their smuttiest routines, in which the pair talk about the worst "job" they ever had, got loaded into a completely different project— a children's version of Black Beauty."

As the 1970s got under way life was changing; we now had a third son Justin and our business began to develop dramatically, opening up new—and lucrative—opportunities. Our engineering team had been expanded, our tea boy had made the jump up to tape op and then to engineer. The studio was producing some amazing people, including Robin Cable, Dave Hentschel and Dennis MacKay.

In 1970 we had installed a disc-cutting suite at Trident after buying the London Disc Cutting Service, which had been based above Rymuse Studios in Bond Street and run by Norman Austin. We moved him and everything to Trident Studios.

It meant that we could now offer the final link in the recording chain. The facility would over time be staffed by some of the best home grown cutting engineers in the business, Bob Hill, Howard "Kipper", Thompson and Ray Staff.

Gus Dudgeon was now producing Elton John. He was great to work with and his band was superb, the whole sound was so percussive and punchy it worked very well. We would go on to record or mix seven albums with Elton over the coming years.

That same year we also built a remix suite, the world's first. By now we had installed a second new desk and 16-track recording equipment in the control room of the studio. This in turn led to long mixing periods for the recordings that left the recording area unusable.

I had begun to see the recording process as being similar to the film industry, where they shot the movie on location or in a studio and then edited it in a different building. I was trying to introduce the same principle, recording in the studio downstairs, moving the tape facilities upstairs to a room with the same acoustics and equipment—with a small adjacent room for adding extra instruments or vocals—as well as some new toys to complete the recording. This room would also allow us to double the studio's output and look after two clients at once.

That year we also installed the world's first Dolby systems in both areas, which raised many eyebrows in the industry, but his systems would go on to become the industry standard. We began to work closely with Ray Dolby on systems for cassette and film recording.

Another new venture was Trident Tape Services, which we started in late 1969 after an approach by a friend of Robert Iggulden. He wanted to know if we could use our audio knowledge for a tape duplication company. I had been following developments in the pre-recorded tape industry and knew it had entered an interesting stage.

There were two systems: tape cassettes and the 8-track cartridge. The latter had been invented in the USA by William Powell Lear (of Lear jet fame) and was aimed at the car audio market. The cartridges ran at 3 3/14 ips, the same speed as radio jingles, which meant that you could play these tapes really loud in your car and still get good audio quality. On the other hand, pre-recorded tapes were still in the hands of Phillips. They ran at half the speed of 8-tracks, and at half the sound quality.

Getting the tape project off the ground was almost as tough as it had been establishing Trident in the first place. We had to source equipment from the US and effectively design a factory from scratch—no easy task considering the lack of industry knowledge at the time. So, once more, we had to improvise.

I found a manufacturing facility in the shape of an old handbag factory in North London, which had a good source of labour. I then put Ron Goodwin, one of our very first members of staff, in charge.

The process meant a lot of trips to America for me as I sought out all the various duplication equipment we needed. Those trips produced a funny story or two.

During one trip I hired a car and travelled to North Hollywood to visit one of the manufacturers. I couldn't find their address, and having driven up and down this long road several times I suddenly saw a police car behind me signalling me to stop.

I pulled over. It was just like a scene from the movies as this cop in aviator sunglasses approached from the side and told me to put my hands on the wheel.

He told me that a local resident had called the cops and said I appeared to be casing the area.

He asked for my driving licence and I duly produced it, cased in the small red book that UK licences were then contained in.

He gave it one look as if to say, "what the fuck is this?"

He then radioed the station to see if my licence was genuine.

Fortunately, all was well. He then asked me where I was trying to get to and explained that it was tricky to find because a freeway cut the street in half.

"I'll take you there, just follow me," he said.

I ended up arriving with a police escort, which surprised the people I was visiting.

Getting the tape factory moving wasn't easy. Inevitably, we had many teething problems, the biggest of which involved the low temperature shrink wrapping machine required to package the finished tapes. We simply couldn't find one.

Then one day I remembered that there was a food packing plant near where I lived in Hoddesdon. I gave them a ring and asked them about how they wrapped their products. So we ended up shrink-wrapping cartridges in a cheese-packing machine. Later we used a modified cigarette-packaging machine.

The plant was soon up and running, however, and presenting new business opportunities. One day I came across an Elton John cartridge manufactured by one of the major labels. It had been recorded at Trident so I knew what the sound should be like—and it wasn't anywhere near the quality. So I went to see Dick James, who was Elton's manager at the time.

"This product doesn't represent your artist," I said, handing him the cartridge.

"It sounds okay in my Rolls Royce," he said. "Could you make me a better one?"

"Bloody right I could," I said.

A few days later I went back with our version to him and won the contract to manufacture all of Elton's work. Of course it didn't hurt that we were the first duplicator, and, I think, the only one at that time to have a mastering suite in the factory staffed by studio personnel. It was a measure of how good we were that Ray Dolby used our factory to develop the Dolby system for cassettes.

Of course, there were problems. There always are!

One day I received a phone call from my old friend David Betteridge, who had left Island Records to become chief exec at RCA, for whom we were manufacturing a massive double album of Elvis hits for the Christmas market.

He wasn't happy. He said that although this album was not due for release until November and we had all of the stock, a member of his staff had seen a copy of this tape on sale in Petticoat Lane. I told him I'd sort it out and launched an investigation.

To my horror I found out that some of the night shift were running their own copies and storing them in the Ladies toilet cistern for one of our drivers to collect the next day. I had no choice but to inform the police and bring charges against the relevant staff.

We were producing all sorts of different titles at this time, including the most controversial—and funny—album of the day, the infamous Derek & Clive recordings that Island had done with Peter Cook and Dudley Moore.

Somehow one of their smuttiest routines, in which the pair talk about the worst "job" they ever had, got loaded into a completely different project—a children's version of Black Beauty. I had to take a very embarrassing phone call from the producer of the children's books.

Such setbacks aside, there was no doubt about it: the company was now making money and producing very good financial results, particularly in the new areas where we were beating all our major competitors with extremely high quality recordings and a low reject rate.

~

Back at the studio a huge range of artists were now heading to St. Anne's Court. Charisma and Tony Stratton-Smith, with whom we'd quickly forged a great working relationship, were sending us most of their acts. Aside from Van der Graaf Generator we worked with Rare Bird, Lindisfarne, and Genesis. Tony's main producer had brought them over, a former DJ at the Speakeasy called John Anthony. John was a big character and loved the atmosphere at the studio. That love rubbed off on his artists. Genesis' drummer Phil Collins quickly began to regard Trident as his bolthole in Soho whenever he was in town. He'd come in and sit in the lobby reading the papers, even on days when the band weren't recording. There was a real "artists' colony" kind of feel evolving. People would help each other out, chipping in opinions and playing on each other's records.

More and more artists from the States were coming over as well. Frank Zappa popped over here in 1970 to record Chunga's Revenge with, amongst many others Ringo Starr.

Despite the bust ups, The Beatles remained part of the Trident "family" John Lennon recorded his Plastic Ono Band material with us, while George Harrison worked on his solo album All Things Must Pass as well. They were some of the biggest fans of the creative melting pot that was Trident. They loved the fact that everyone and anyone could have some input, even the secretaries.

That was typified when my PA, a lovely lady called Brit Marie Young, was filling in for a sick colleague and working on reception one day while George was recording. Just like when the boys had first come over to record "Hey Jude", George liked to create an atmosphere in the studio. So, there were incense sticks burning in the studio and in the reception.

As George kept running up and down the stairs between the studio and the control room, Brit couldn't help hearing the music that was coming out. It was "My Sweet Lord".

"I hope you will release this song as a single, because it is wonderful and I'm sure it will be a hit," she said to George.

Elsewhere she'd have been told to mind her own business, or, in some cases, sacked on the spot. Not at Trident. George looked at her and said, "Do you really think so?"

He was too nice a guy to be patronizing. I have no doubt that he really meant it.

~

As with all families, of course, some of our members were growing up and beginning to think about flying the Trident nest. In particular, our sound engineers were becoming so skilled and so successful that they wanted to move up the musical ladder.

Ken Scott, for instance, had become one of the most accomplished practitioners of his art in London. But he was growing sick of situations where if he came up with an idea in the control room, producers would put it to the artist as if it was their own; it didn't go down well, of course, in which case they said, "Oh, don't worry, it was only Ken's idea. I didn't think it would work."

It was the same thing with another engineer, Robin Cable. Robin had struck up a really good relationship with Gus Dudgeon, but he and Elton John had hit it off especially well.

Elton had recorded his first album, Empty Sky, at his manager Dick James' own studios in London in the early months of 1969. Subsequently Gus Dudgeon had big plans for Elton, who with his writing partner Bernie Taupin was crafting songs at a prolific rate.

They decided that Elton's second album, called simply Elton John, needed a bigger, more sophisticated studio. So, in January 1970 he came to us. Gus Dudgeon produced it with Robin Cable as his sound engineer. Elton had loved the studio. He'd been back again within weeks, in March, to record another album, Tumbleweed Connection. He was back for a third time in August 1971 to do Madman Across The Water, working with Robin once more.

Trident would eventually record or mix seven of Elton's albums.

~

So in late 1970 we formed a company called Neptune for Roy Baker and Robin Cable, and another called Nereus with Ken Scott.

Robin was working with Dina Gillespie and Chris De Burgh. Ken was working with David Bowie along with Roy Baker—who had worked with Tony Visconti, The Rolling Stones, Frank Zappa, and T.Rex. They had all approached us with the idea of becoming producers at some point. We were all for it and suggested managing them in separate companies. Of course, they could not rely on production income entirely at this time, so we structured a deal which kept everybody on salary and available to the studio with fees repayable from any royalties generated over time.

Ken was the first to take off. By now David Bowie and Tony Visconti had decided to go their separate ways. Ken and Bowie got on very well and had been talking about the direction he should head in next. At that point David didn't have a recording contract. After talking to Ken, he asked him to produce his new album, Hunky Dory.

The piano in the studio was becoming an integral part of our success. It was a Bechstein, which I leased from a company called Jake Samuel Pianos, a leading piano dealer in London. Everyone loved it and it had begun to be featured on records from Elton, Carly Simon, Genesis, David Bowie, and Supertramp. Alongside the piano we also had a Hammond C3 Organ, a Fender Rhodes piano and a Mellotron all tucked away in the studios and available to be used if needed.

Our "house pianist" often manned the bench, a young, classically trained musician named Rick Wakeman. Also a founding member of the band Yes, Rick had played the new, electronic instrument known as the Mellotron on Bowie's song "Space Oddity", picking up £9 for his work. Bowie really liked him, and he and Ken put him to work on the Hunky Dory album next. Rick and the Bechstein featured on a couple of its standout tracks, "Changes" and "Life on Mars?".

~

As all this was going on, we were still developing Trident on the technical front. Part of our appeal lay in the fact that we were pioneering both new recording equipment and new techniques to go with them. People like Herb Alpert were coming over to look at what we were doing. I remember him looking in disbelief at our studio, which in American terms was quite tiny. He couldn't believe that we were getting such massive, complicated, rich sounds from a small studio in an alleyway in Soho.

The technical side of things meant that I had to be careful about diversifying too much—at least for the time being.

There were plenty of temptations to do otherwise. I'd already been asked to think about managing a band called Deep Purple, a heavy rock act from Hertford who'd been brought to us. They'd made a breakthrough with a version of "Hush" and had, in Richie Blackmore, a really impressive lead guitarist. Rock acts like them and Led Zeppelin were changing the face of the industry. But I'd said no. I'd had a taste of management when I'd very briefly looked after a band called Unit Four Plus Two back when I still had the record shop. Of course I had experience before that looking after my own band, The Hunters, but I wasn't ready to manage a band.

As things took off, however, I did come to the conclusion that we needed an A&R man.

The idea was that we would try and build up a roster of acts, record an album with each of them, and then try to set up a production deal with a record company. That way we'd get our own label. This approach had worked already in the States and I felt sure we could pull it off, provided, of course, we could get the right acts. It would be the A&R guy's job to find and nurture those acts for us.

I knew that John Anthony over at Charisma had ambitions in this direction. So we asked him if he wanted to join us. He agreed and soon he was scouting around London and the rest of the country on the lookout for unsigned acts.

Within the first few months John brought three acts to us. The first was a singer he'd found in an Irish club, Eugene Wallace. He was Irish, from Limerick originally, and was in the Joe Cocker mould. He had a big voice. He'd played at the big concert for Bangladesh at The Oval in 1971 with The Who, which was where John had seen him, I think.

The second was Mark Ashton, who had been the drummer and singer in Rare Bird, a Charisma act that had disbanded. They'd had a big hit in 1969 with a song called "Sympathy", but they'd fizzled out after that.

It was the third act that would make the real impact—not just on John, me and Trident, but on the entire music world.

Six

Meet The Queenies

"The bad news was that—heavily influenced by Freddie—they'd chosen a new name. I nearly choked on my coffee when John Anthony first told me what it was: Queen."

I was sitting in my office one day when I got a call from my brother Barry down in the studio.

"Norman, come down and have a listen to something will you?" he said.

I finished off what I was doing and headed down. Barry was there, sitting at the mixing desk with Roy Baker and John Anthony.

"So what's up, what have you got?" I asked.

John explained to me that he'd just been up at the De Lane Lea recording studio in Wembley. We'd been thinking about getting some new recording consoles and they had some kit that had just been installed. John and Roy had gone up to check it out.

They had arrived to discover there was a band laying down demo tracks for the engineers. There was nothing unusual about that. That's what you did then. You'd bring in a band to test the studio. You'd record demos of them all day for free so that you could road test the equipment, and at the end of it all the band would get a tape of the session. It was a good arrangement for both sides.

The minute he saw the band John recognised them. They were known as Smile, and had been formed a few years earlier by some students in London. John had recorded them at Trident for the Mercury label back in 1969. The lead guitarist was an astronomy student from Imperial College called Brian May; the bassist and singer was a guy called Tim Staffell, who was at Ealing Art College; and the drummer was a biology student called Roger Taylor.

They'd gigged around London a lot and landed a one-off recording deal with Mercury. They'd recorded three promotional tracks with us in June 1969, but they'd never even been published. After another failed attempt at recording for Mercury, they had gone their separate ways—or so John thought. It turned out that they'd stuck together and reshaped the band.

Tim Staffell had been replaced by this little Indian looking guy with a big, quite operatic voice. And they had a new bass player as well.

As they'd settled into the studio, John had said to Roy, "That's interesting, they've got a new singer. I like the sound of that."

John and Roy had asked Smile for a copy of their demo. We stuck it on inside the control room and had a listen. It was raw, but there was definitely something there. The standard of musicianship was very high, and there was a real energy to it.

"That does sound interesting," I said.

John mentioned that they were playing a gig a couple of nights later. "It's at a nurses' dance in Norwood," he said, which raised a few laughs.

I was about to fly out to the States on a scouting mission. We were thinking of buying a studio out there. So I asked Barry to go along and have a listen. I trusted his judgment.

"I'll catch up when I get back," I said.

A few days later I got back and asked him how they were.

"Very good," he said.

We decided to get them in and have a chat about recording them.

~

The four guys who came into my office a couple of weeks later were an intriguing mix of characters.

I recognised the drummer Roger Taylor immediately. I remembered sticking my head in to the control room when Smile had been recording a couple of years earlier and being impressed by his drumming. He was from Cornwall and was a really good looking kid. He was also a rock star from top to toe. He had long, blonde hair and a real easy-going charm. I could tell that the girls were going to go for him in a big way.

Brian May was a tall lad with a mane of curls. He was quiet and a little introverted but clearly very intelligent. He was studying astrophysics at Imperial College and told us that he'd built his own guitar with his dad, a draughtsman with the Ministry of Aviation. The bass player, John Deacon, was also on the quiet side. He too had a scientific background, specifically in electronics. I could tell that he was a strong influence, one of those stabilising forces that all bands needed, and that this one in particular was going to need.

I say this because I could tell almost right away that the fourth and most distinctive member of the group was going to be high maintenance.

His real name, I would learn later, was Farokh Bulsara. He was from a Parsi family, born in Zanzibar and educated in India. The family had immigrated to England when he was a teenager in the mid-sixties when, settling in Feltham. He was a talented artist and had gone to Ealing Art College, where he'd got a diploma in art and graphic design. It had been there that he'd gotten to know another student named Tim Staffell.

Freddie had studied music at school and was a gifted singer and pianist. He could also play other instruments—including the guitar—I would later discover. He'd been in a couple of bands in his late teens. The first was called Ibex, and later there was Wreckage. The latter were strongly influenced by the heavy rock of Jimi Hendrix, Freddie's hero at the time, but the group didn't last. After that he'd joined a band called Sour Milk Sea, but they'd broken up after one of the band members decided to quit and take all his equipment with him.

So when Tim Staffell had left Smile he'd wasted no time in suggesting that his mate Farokh take over. The singer jumped at the chance and immediately gave himself a slightly more rock 'n' roll name: Freddie Mercury. I loved the name, I had to say. He was clearly a really talented young man. He was charming, acted a bit shy and reserved at times, and spoke in quite a posh, mannered voice. When he relaxed and opened up he had a very sharp, quite sarcastic sense of humour and spoke at a hundred miles an hour, flicking his hands and waving his arms around as he did so.

We sat down in my office with John Anthony and just talked a bit about their backgrounds, their hopes and dreams. Freddie did a lot of the talking, along with Roger, who exuded confidence. Brian chipped in a little and John was virtually silent. I sensed a slight nervousness in all four of them, but Freddie in particular was a real bundle of competing emotions. One minute he would be very precise and specific, the next he was quite confused. I could tell he was a volatile character and that he was going to need a very firm rein. That wasn't a concern to me, however. There were managers around who could handle him.

The biggest obstacle at that point, at least for me, was their name. They'd rightly decided to ditch Smile as their moniker. That band hadn't worked. It needed to be consigned to the past.

That was the good news, the bad news was that—heavily influenced by Freddie—they'd chosen a new name. I nearly choked on my coffee when John Anthony first told me what it was: Queen.

Back in the early 1970s, the word had very strong gay connotations. And back then the world wasn't as enlightened and accepting of homosexuality as it is today. We were worried that it would be a real turn off, especially given the way the band looked. Freddie apparently had a girlfriend, a girl from Kensington market called Mary, but his very flamboyant manner could easily have been mistaken for campiness. It worried me.

But it was clear from that first meeting that all four of them were strong-minded individuals. And they made it pretty clear at that stage that the name wasn't up for negotiation.

That was their prerogative at that point. We didn't have a deal with them—and nor would we for a while, at least.

After talking to Barry, I agreed to offer the boys—or the Queenies, as we very quickly christened them—a loose kind of arrangement where we would start working with them on some material. The idea was that once we had some good songs we'd go shopping around town for a recording deal.

The boys immediately jumped at the offer. After all Trident was an international entity!

People often ask me why we didn't snap them up straight away, and the answer is simple. They were nowhere near the finished article then. When we first said we'd take them on they only had two tracks to play us. That was all, just a couple demos from De Lane Lea. They had some other stuff from Smile, but that was irrelevant because they'd had two different players in the band then. And they'd gotten nowhere.

What we'd seen personally all looked good. And we could tell they were excellent musicians and bright lads. But there were plenty of bands around with good musicians. They needed to work at it.

Fortunately, we were in a unique position to help them.

The studio wasn't in use twenty-four hours a day. There were times when the facilities were "dark", sitting there doing nothing, usually from around 2 a.m. onwards. At other times, bands would shelve their recording plans on short notice. I had a word with Barry and we agreed that we should give our new discoveries the run of the studio during these empty periods.

So we said to Freddie, Brian, Roger, and John, "We'll give you this down time in the studio to see what you can do. Use the studio when it's empty and we'll see what you produce."

Over the years people have accused me of being a skinflint for doing things that way. There has been a lot of rubbish written by people who didn't know what they were talking about. Years later, Queen themselves had a moan about it. Why didn't we treat them like a normal band and let them record during the normal hours of the day? Why didn't we send them off to another studio? Why did we behave like cheapskates?

These accusations have always annoyed me. Not only do they paint Trident and me in an unfair light, they couldn't be further from the truth.

To begin with, the band was still very raw and rather rough around the edges. We needed to find out if they were as good as they thought they were. and whether they really did have they have the material? All we had to go on was the De Lane Lee demo and our gut feelings.

Secondly, the Queen sound—driven by Roger Taylor's drums, John Deacon's bass, and Freddie's operatic voice—was huge. On top of this the Queenies wanted John Anthony and Roy Baker to do the production. In fact, almost all of the engineering team worked with the band on their first album, including Ken, Robin & Roy, and Mike Stone.

So Trident was really the only place for the band to experiment. Where else could they record to 16-track at that time? Where else could they get the chance to experiment with the best engineers and equipment in the world? The answer to that was simple: nowhere.

I don't know of any other band that has had an opportunity like that. They were still very raw, far from the finished product. They learned their craft during those sessions, taking advantage of an un-fettered chance at developing their skills.

People have also argued that this arrangement didn't cost Trident a thing. Again, this is rubbish.

We didn't just give Freddie, Brian, Roger, and John a set of keys and say "help yourself".

The studio had to be operated in the normal way, with a full complement of staff, no different than for any normal session.

What the process did achieve was that it sped things up. Another demo studio would not have had the equipment to open up the band's ideas. We also saved them the whole process of demoing—with all of the usual laments that they could have done it better with the right equipment—only to have to record everything again. Everything could be done in-house.

But it wasn't free, far from it. In fact we were paying a lot of the staff overtime. The cost of these sessions was nothing, however, compared to what we'd be spending on Queen down the road.

From my standpoint, it was a big risk, one we believed in, but the whole affair could have turned out to be a disaster.

~

One of-the first things we did was sort out some decent instruments for them. Roger needed a new drum kit, for instance. They also needed a PA system for the gigs that we wanted them to perform in order to polish up their live act. That wasn't cheap. The only one who didn't need any new equipment was Brian, who was devoted to his homemade guitar, and quite understandably. The "Red Special" as it came to be known had its own distinctive sound, and was famously crafted by him and his father. I think that parts of it came from an old mantelpiece, and I'm quite certain Brian still uses it today.

Freddie, I quickly discovered, also liked to spend money. Clothes, in particular, he felt were very important to the band. He'd often tell John to wear something different, especially if they were going to do a gig.

He still worked in Kensington Market at this point, so he would come in wearing all sorts of creations from the stalls there. He would strut around the place, talking in that very distinctive and penetrating voice of his. Freddie had a way of getting people to do things for him. He used to tell a story about how he once worked at a warehouse near Heathrow airport, which was close to his home. It involved a lot of heavy lifting, something that Freddie wasn't exactly designed to do. His workmates commented once on what "delicate hands" he had. Freddie told them that he was a singer and that he was just "filling in time" while he was at work. Soon his co-workers were doing the lion's share of Freddie's work on top of their own, as the story goes.

His larger-than-life personality was soon rubbing off on everyone else.

Roy Baker spent a lot of time overseeing production on the tracks the band were laying down. After a while he started mimicking Freddie's rather camp affectations. Soon everyone else was imitating The Queenies, as we all affectionately called them by now.

As Howard "Kipper" Thompson recalled later, "Suddenly everyone was mincing around, calling each other 'dearie' and talking as if we were all locked in some dreadful Larry Grayson episode."

Roy Baker very much liked the band's music, which was based on fairytales and fantasy, and had been influenced by strange artists like Richard Dadd, a resident of a Victorian mental asylum. Kipper, however, was very particular about the music he liked, and he just couldn't get his head around songs like "My Fairy King", "Great King Rat", and "Jesus".

"Sitting there hitting 'record' and endlessly rewinding spools of tape while being hammered by this stuff began to feel like torture," he said years later. After a while he begged our studio manager at the time, Penny Kramer, to put him to use somewhere else in the building. So, we confined him to a little cupboard-like space on the third floor, where he was put to use copying masters, tapes, and stereo mixes for us. Unfortunately for him, he would soon find himself working more and more on the band that he was so desperate to avoid.

Seven

Creative Differences

" One would stop, one would go right, one would go left, and the other one would go straight ahead. That was the way they were. "

By 1972 we were welcoming some of the biggest artists in the world to Trident. Richard Perry, who was one of the most influential producers on the American scene at the time, was convinced that London was where it was at and was sending more and more people over to us. He even went public and said that British producers were "more creative" than Americans. That pissed off a few people stateside apparently, but it didn't worry me. We reaped the benefits—big time. People like Leon Russell, Frank Zappa, Mamma Cass, Santana, Wayne Newton, Johnny Mathis, Sammy Davis, and the Rowan & Martin's Laugh-In team travelled over to record, remix, or cut their masters at Trident.

Not all of them enjoyed the experience, of course. Neil Diamond didn't like the place, for instance, but he was in a minority, Chris loved him and when he was booked in she travelled from Hertfordshire and by the time she arrived at the studio he had left!

Mamma Cass in particular reinforced Richard Perry's message, singing our praises in the press. She had broken away from The Mammas & Pappas and begun a solo career. She was a perfectionist. She knew what she wanted. She always used to crochet during recording sessions, although she complained that the lighting was too subdued sometimes.

When she was recording her album The Road is No Place for a Lady, she said that she loved it at Trident, especially compared to her last US studio. "The Hollywood studio I did my last album in was more like an aircraft hangar," she said. At Trident it was different. "I can look up at my producer and see if he's angry, happy, or merely fallen asleep."

That wasn't quite as unusual as it might sound.

Another artist that Richard worked with was Harry Nilsson. He recorded his breakthrough album Nilsson Schmilsson with us in 1971, which of course contained "Without You" and "Coconut" this album was a major wonderful piece of work by all concerned and it earned Trident and Robin Cable many awards, including a Grammy nomination. He then returned a year later to record the follow up Son Of Schmilsson with a great line up of artists, including Ringo Starr. I'll never forget his time with us.

He'd landed at Heathrow late at night but had got one of his team on the phone to the studio saying he was heading straight there and needed some musicians for an all night session.

Poor old Rick Wakeman had been fast asleep in his bed when the phone went at something like 2 a.m. It was the session's fixer David Katz.

He asked Rick whether he could make it in. Rick hadn't been in bed long and had another session at nine that same morning, so at first he said no. But then David reminded him that a session at that time of the night would pay him something like £200, a small fortune in the 1970's.

Rick was soon dragging himself out of bed and into the studio. He arrived to be greeted by Harry Nilsson and his entourage.

Rick went straight into the studio, where he started working on something with Nilsson. He could tell Nilsson was the worse for wear after his flight, but he said nothing. He was just the pianist, nothing to do with him!

After just a few minutes doodling around, Nilsson said he was going up to the control room to have a listen to what they'd laid down.

Rick just sat at the piano and waited—and waited and waited. After about half an hour of this he thought he'd better have a look to see what was going on. There were no lights in the control room and no one was answering when he tried to talk to them via the mike.

He went up the stairs to the control room. The room was in semi-darkness and empty, apart from the figure of Nilsson, who was slumped on top of the mixing desk snoring away. He'd just passed out apparently, exhausted by a mixture of jetlag and—knowing him,—a load of booze. It was the easiest £200 Rick had ever earned.

Nilsson was great fun to work with though. You never knew what was going to happen. Like a lot of artists, he liked to create an atmosphere in the studio. With The Beatles it had been incense and plants. With Harry it was white curtains. He insisted we have them hanging everywhere. He also liked to have a fair bit of booze around the place too.

Harry pulled out all the stops during the recording of Son of Schmilsson. Peter Frampton was in his backing band, but he also recruited a mini army of other musicians to chip in, including Ringo Star, Nicky Hopkins, Ray Cooper, Lowell George of Little Feat, and even Richard Perry on some percussion, the list of musicians amounted to about twenty five, all among the best in the world. The biggest production, however, was on a rather grim song called "I'd Rather Be Dead". I think the chorus line was "I'd rather be dead, than wet the bed", so to make it sound really authentic Harry had asked for the music fixer David Katz to get hold of an octogenarian choir. Somehow he'd found one, a group called the Stepney and Pinner choir club. They were accompanied by the Henry Krein Quartet. That turned into a really crazy scene. We had a couple of dozen of these elderly biddies in the studio and everyone was drinking sherry. They were all soused.

How we managed to record the track I've no idea.

As they left, I'll never forget, this eighty-six-year-old guy with a wooden leg came up to Harry Nilsson and said to him, "See you on the next album Harry." Priceless. .

Some of the more eccentric acts were fun to work with. Others weren't, however.

Our main disc cutting engineers were Ray Staff, Bob Hill, and David Bowie's old mate, Kipper.

The longest night of Kipper's life came when Cat Stevens booked the studio to record and master a single from his new album Foreigner.

He and the engineer had thought it would take a couple of hours, maximum. But they hadn't counted on Cat Stevens' legendary perfectionist streak.

The album was a big departure for Steve, as some people were allowed to call him. After four massively successful albums with Mona Bone Jakon, Tea for the Tillerman, Teaser and the Firecat, and Catch Bull at Four, he'd broken away from his collaborators and tried something new. He was living as a tax exile in Brazil at the time as well. He turned up with his own green stereo system, which he set about installing in an empty office down the corridor. He knew everything sounded amazing inside the Trident studio, but wanted to know what it was going to sound like for the ordinary listener on his or her stereo in their living room or bedroom.

Kipper spent the next fourteen hours cutting reference acetates for a song called "The Hurt". It was quite an appropriate title really.

Kipper had a great turn of phrase and he later described the song as "an execrable ditty that had no chance of being a hit single . . . even if it got played on Radio 1 every hour on the hour."

Every time they cut a disc, Steve would come up with a tiny change that he wanted to make. He'd then go and listen to the latest acetate on his own stereo and sometimes even bring it into the main studio to listen again. He drove everyone completely round the twist.

This carried on all through the night. I'd left them to it when I'd gone home. I turned up the following morning to find poor old Kipper looking like he was ready to roll over and die.

From that day forward he said that he loathed Cat Stevens and everything he stood for.

Kipper was typical of the kind of guy we were employing at Trident. He was an avid and knowledgeable music fan. And he'd been prepared to work his way up through the system.

He'd started—of course—as a tea boy, and eventually worked his way through sound engineering to become one of the best disc cutters in the business. We'd had dozens of talented people like this pass through our doors by now. It was a tough, demanding place to work, but if you had the energy and the application you'd make it. It could be something of a baptism of fire, and in one case it turned out to be that quite literally.

One day while Gus Dudgeon was recording with Elton, he and David

Henshall decided they would like some dinner. This was something that came as part of the service. We had a fully equipped kitchen, stocked with all sorts of food and drinks, steaks, burgers, beers, you name it.

On this particular day, the kitchen was being manned by a guy called Peter Fielder, who was at that stage working as a tea boy. Dennis McKay, who was the tape operator, rang up to our kitchen and passed on the order.

"Peter, we'll be ready in a few minutes so can you start frying the steak and chips," he said.

Gus and David got on with whatever they were doing but after a while, they began wondering what had happened. Steak and chips normally took twenty minutes, more than half an hour had passed by now.

Gus could be a grouchy character and he was soon voicing his displeasure.

"What the hell happened to that food?" he said to Dennis.

"I'll find out," he said.

Peter answered the phone sounding sheepish.

"I'm afraid there's going to be a delay with the steak and chips," he said.

"Why?" Dennis asked.

"Because I've set the kitchen on fire."

"What . . ."

Dennis went belting out of the control room door and immediately smelled the smoke. He ran upstairs and found Peter was actually hiding in the corridor.

He'd let the chip pan catch fire and the whole kitchen was now filled with smoke. Fortunately we had plenty of fire extinguishers and Dennis was able to put the blaze out.

Needless to say, Peter wasn't put on cooking duties ever again.

~

In the time that had passed since we'd invited them into the studio, Queen had turned out to be every bit as good—and as demanding— as we'd anticipated. They'd taken advantage and spent a large chunk of down time in the studio. If they'd been with a big label their management would have been tearing their hair out.

They'd often get into the studio at 2 a.m. and work through until the cleaning staff all came in at around 7 a.m. They were a volatile bunch, and there were often arguments. Plates and glasses would be flying across the studio as tempers flared. Freddie, predictably, was often at the centre of the fuss, but so too were Roger and Brian. Roger, in particular, could get quite worked up. But the more I got to know the band and their music, the less I was surprised at the eruptions. It was part of who they were.

To begin with, their music was very demanding because it was so intricate. The material they were working on included some of the stuff we'd heard from the De Lane Lea sessions, including "Keep Yourself Alive", "Liar", "The Night Comes Down", and "Jesus". But there were also these slightly bizarre pieces that drew on poetry like "Great King Rat" and "My Fairy King", which had lines from Robert Browning's "The Pied Piper".

(It was while they were working on the last of these that I discovered where Freddie got the idea for his surname. It was a line from "My Fairy King", which he'd apparently been writing back in his days with Ibex. It went "Mother Mercury, look what they've done to me.")

There were all sorts of weird and wonderful influences there, and the music was really complex, with high-pitched vocal harmonies and all sorts of effects going on, so getting it right took a lot of work. If someone got something wrong it really threw a spanner in the works.

But they were also absolute perfectionists. Things had to be one hundred percent right, otherwise they wouldn't be happy. They'd spend days and nights working on the vocal harmonies. They were also really concerned about their sound, and in particular the tonal quality of Brian's guitar, for instance. Freddie and Brian used to sit at the mixing desk studying the phasing on the stereo mixes. They'd sit there for hours twiddling away, with Robin or Roy trying to get the smallest things just right.

But they were also a nervous band. There was a lot of highly-strung energy in there. I think all of them, with the possible exception of John, lived on their nerves at that time.

Arguments would start about the tiniest little detail. They'd start screaming and shouting, waving their arms around and chucking things. Often you'd walk into one of their sessions and think they'd been trying to kill each other. Sometimes it would blow over in a few minutes, but at other times it would last longer. They would then stew on it, not talking to each other for a day or two. They'd always sort it out, however. It wasn't personal, it was about the work. The more I looked at them the more I began to see that the nervous energy was part of what made them work as a band. We now had some great workable material, and so we began to look at a recording deal. We'd also talked to them about a publishing deal.

It turned out that Tony Stratton-Smith at Charisma had already approached them, but they'd turned him down. He hadn't offered them enough money to even buy equipment. They might have thought we were being tight, but they were smart enough to know that we were actually spending a small fortune on them.

They also knew we could back up the offer with the studios. We were a bigger, more sophisticated operation, in their eyes at least. The discussions were going fine, but then, to my surprise and alarm, they'd also asked us about managing them.

Freddie was quite insistent about it for some reason. "We don't want anyone else managing us. We want Trident," he'd say. This didn't make much sense to me for a couple of reasons.

Firstly, I didn't see us in the management business, looking after the day-to-day life of artists, especially such highly-strung ones. But more importantly, I thought it was a conflict of interests. There wouldn't be a problem if they remained a small band. But that wasn't the intention, and I always had a feeling they were going to make it big. The interests of a record company and the interests of a band weren't always going to be the same. In fact, they were almost certain to become very different.

It slowed things down for a while, although, of course, it was all fairly academic until we got some product to be able to land ourselves a distribution and label deal.

With that in mind I was about to visit the States on business and had arranged to go and stay with a friend of mine called Jack Nelson. He'd worked for Blue Thumb Records and was now with MGM, and was very well connected in the business. I'd known him for a couple of years, having met him through Chris Odell at Apple Records. I hoped he might be able to help us open a few doors.

I played him the tracks we'd recorded with Queen, Eugene Wallace, and Skin Alley. Jack was particularly impressed by Queen. He really liked their sound, not just Brian's guitar and Freddie's vocals, but the power of the band as a whole. He was really keen to try to shop them around on our behalf, and we agreed on a deal accordingly.

He moved over to London to work for us in June of 1972 and immediately began knocking on people's doors, trying to get Trident a recording deal.

At first Jack was met with blank faces. They just didn't get Queen. Jack was working for Trident, so he also needed to try to find a manager for Queen, although we still weren't keen on having them in-house.

He had a friend who knew a top American manager called Dee Anthony. He was in London at the time so Jack asked to see him. He was at home in Hampstead one night when the phone rang telling him to come to Anthony's hotel in Park Lane.

Jack played him Queen's tapes, but Dee wasn't too impressed. "I've got a band called Humble Pie who are going to be much bigger than this," he told Jack.

That wasn't such a smart prediction, but what he said next was.

"You should manage them yourself," he said, to Jack's surprise.

"Why do you say that?" he asked.

"Because anyone who's prepared to drive to meetings at midnight to try and sell a band is already managing that band anyway," he said.

That really made Jack stop and think. On the drive back up to Hampstead, Jack concluded that Dee was right. So he agreed to manage the band on our behalf. As he figured it, what was there to lose?

When we put this to Freddie and the boys they agreed pretty much straight away. They wanted us to manage them, so they'd got their way.

Jack was a very smart guy, and he quickly "got" Queen and their unique personalities.

He told me once that they reminded him of The Beatles in the sense that they were all total opposites of each other. They were, as he put it, "like the four points of the compass."

On the one hand you had Freddie, who was hugely talented but extremely complicated. We were all pretty certain that he was gay. But he was actually living in Kensington with his girlfriend, a really nice girl called Mary Austin, who had been manageress at the famous Biba boutique. She actually did a lot to keep him on the straight and narrow, if you'll excuse the pun.

Brian May, by contrast, was a kind of mad scientist. He was also very, very talented, but Jack saw that he was also a bit of a contradiction. In life he was a bit scatterbrained and was forever jumping around trying different things. But in the studio he was incredibly focused on his music, right down to the tiniest details.

John, as was often the case with bass players, was the solid citizen. He was obviously an extremely talented student and would in fact go on to get a first-class degree in electronics. But his down-to-earth manner was also a great asset to the band. He was kind of the anchor that gave the others some kind of stability.

Finally, Roger was another one with a complex side to him. He too was really bright, but he could get very emotional in the studio. He wanted success as much, if not more, than any of the band, except perhaps Freddie.

All in all, Jack thought they were the smartest band he'd ever come across. But, as personalities, they were just so diverse. As he rather beautifully put it once, when he got to an airport with them, one would stop, one would go right, one would go left, and the other one would go straight ahead. That was the way they were.

For the immediate future, however, we needed Queen to stick together. We wanted them to keep developing material and releasing an album. But the studios were extremely busy at the time, and they had to hang around a lot. Luckily there was no shortage of other work for them to do.

By now some of the biggest producers in the world were coming to us. None was bigger than Phil Spector, the man who invented the "wall of sound" in the sixties and had been responsible for some of the biggest hits of that decade. He'd worked with George Harrison on his Concert for Bangladesh, and on Harrison's first solo album All Things Must Pass before that.

He also worked with us recording his then-wife Ronnie on tracks for the Apple label.

Our producers were in awe of Spector when he came in, partly because of the reputation he had. We'd heard the stories about him being strange, but he seemed okay to me. He was pedantic and a perfectionist but, hey, what did we expect? Robin Cable had been asked to work with Spector. He'd was fascinated by the experience and had been determined to understand the magic behind the "wall of sound".

Afterwards we were talking and he said he thought he knew how to do something similar. So I said to him, "Why don't you have a go, do something with the same feel to it?" He jumped at the chance, and immediately picked out a couple of songs. The first was "I Can Hear Music"—by Jeff Barry, Ellie Greenwich and Spector himself—which had been a hit for both The Ronettes and The Beach Boys. The other one was "Goin' Back"—written by Gerry Goffin and Carole King— which had charted for both Dusty Springfield and The Byrds. All he needed now was someone to sing them. He found the answer sitting under our noses, flicking through magazines as he waited impatiently for some more studio time to come free for Queen.

Everyone knew that Freddie had an amazing voice. He had an extraordinary vocal range. He could do everything from a deep growling sort of bass, to a beautiful tenor, to a high-pitched "coloratura" soprano. It was amazing to hear. Robin asked me what I thought, and I shrugged my shoulders. "Why not?" Apart from anything else, it might give the boys the break they needed.

John was still studying at university by day, so Robin got Roger in on drums and Brian in on guitar. They were hanging around a lot then too.

Freddie, Roger, and Brian really put their heart and soul into recording with Robin, as I'd expected. The results were really good, certainly from a technical point of view. Robin was right; he had worked out how to create that intense, thunderous "wall of sound". And Freddie's voice was certainly good.

Our only problem at the end was what to do with it? There was no obvious way of marketing it, and we didn't want to release it with Freddie, Roger, and Brian's name on it. That would interfere with the plans we had for Queen. So, with Robin's agreement, the record was released under our Trident EMI deal in 1973 under the name of Larry Lurex. It died.

Little did we, or anyone else, know we'd recorded something that would—in time—become a collector's item.

Eight

Doing Alright

"Don't worry. We can make a band out of this. It's just going to need an awful lot of work."

Whenever anyone asked him, Freddie Mercury used to say there was no question in his mind that Queen would be a success. "There was never a doubt, darling, never," he'd say with an imperious wave of his hand. "I just knew we would make it, and told everyone who asked just that."

The second half of that statement was true: he did tell anyone who asked that they would make it. Always. But the first half was an entirely different matter. There were doubts that they'd make it. Lots and lots of them.

As 1972 wore on, Jack Nelson was working overtime trying to generate some interest in the band, as well as our other artists, Eugene Wallace, Mark Ashton, and Headstone. But he was getting nowhere.

Some were interested in Queen individually, but not the other two. But we weren't interested in splitting our roster of artists up: it was all three acts or nothing. We were trying to set up a distribution/label deal.

By the summer of 1972 we'd been turned down by most labels. Jack targeted EMI as the next company to try.

The label was looking to break into the rock market and were keen on Queen. But again we said it was all our acts or nothing. As far as EMI was concerned, it was nothing—at least for now. But they told us there was a lot going on at the company, with new labels being created, so we should stay in touch.

Queen weren't fazed by the rejections. They were writing a lot of new material and were pushing us to let them loose on the studio to record it. There was no doubt that Freddie, in particular, had huge ambition for the band. He was already developing much more than their music. He was trying to create a Queen "brand". Clothes were hugely important to him. So he'd persuaded me to let him commission a top fashion designer, Zandra Rhodes, to make some costumes for him and the rest of the band. It cost us a few hundred quid.

He'd also designed a logo for the band. Well, it was more like a coat of arms, actually.

Freddie was a talented artist. He'd studied art at college and had spent a lot of time doing drawings of his hero, Jimi Hendrix. After college, he'd run a stall with Roger Taylor selling prints of his art at Kensington Market, which was the real centre of the fashion scene at that time. He'd drawn on his talent to come up with this logo, very much like the crest or coat of arms of some aristocratic family.

He was fascinated by astrology, and the design revolved around the four band members' star signs. Roger and John were both Leos, Brian was a Cancer, and Freddie was a Virgo. He designed this flamboyant crest with two lions—representing Leo—holding a large, letter Q. The Q had a crown on top. Either side were a crab—for Cancer—and two fairies, for the Virgo member of the band, of course. Dominating the design was a striking drawing of a Phoenix, the symbol of hope rising from the ashes.

As all this was going on, the band were pestering us to start paying them a decent salary. So we agreed to advance them a wage of £100 (c.£1,300) a week net of tax.

It was generous. Other bands like the Rolling Stones or The Beatles weren't on wages prior to the release of their first recordings. They had to rely on the income from their gigs.

The boys all lived in rented accommodation, so this was enough to cover their living expenses and a bit more, we figured. They moaned about it, of course. But I reminded them how much money we were already risking.

Despite our occasional differences, we were all happy with the way things were going, so much so, in fact, that we were ready to sign a deal with them. It was a three-contract deal. The management contract was with Trident Audio Productions, the publishing recording deal was with Neptune productions and the publishing contract was with Trident/Feldman Music, later to become part of EMI. The agreements were signed on the 1st of November, 1972. The deal also reflected the advances that we had paid to them to date and equipment purchases of £6,000 (c.£71,000). We didn't realise it at the time, but it was a pioneering deal, the first between a band and an independent production company, although we still had not yet found someone to release the band's first album!

We didn't have a big celebration. As far as we were concerned we were merely giving a break to a band who we thought could bring something fresh and original to the music scene. So we just went across the road to The Ship. I can't remember exactly, but I think Freddie had a gin and tonic and the others had a beer.

The Ship had become even more of a rock 'n' roll meeting place. The Rolling Stones had an office nearby on Wardour Street, as did The Who. You'd sometimes see them in there. Tony Stratton-Smith treated the place like his office. He would sit there all day on a long bench, holding court. I'd come in and he'd say, "Ah, just the man, I want to talk to you, I've got two more acts I want to put in the studio."

Finally putting pen to paper and signing a deal with Queen really turned the heat up for me and Jack Nelson. There was even more onus on us to get them that elusive record deal. We knew there was only one way to do that. And that was to promote and push the living daylights out of the band.

And so it was that, on a dark and rather grim early winter's night at the beginning of November 1972 that I left the studio and headed down the Kings Road to a large venue called The Pheasantry, where we'd organised a showcase concert for Queen.

It was a big, airy old place. Arriving there I saw it was full of familiar faces, a lot of them people we'd invited from the record companies. I got myself a drink and started to mingle.

I could smell a bit of tension in the air. I had a word with Jack and his new assistant Dave Thomas. They told me that the sound equipment had arrived late and the band were still trying to get it right. I could see that they'd called on the expert electrical services of John Deacon.

After a while the lights went down and the band came out. Not only was it the first time a lot of these record executives were seeing Queen live, it was the first time for me, too.

There was no doubt the band looked the part. They were wearing black and white outfits, with tight, silk trousers, and flowing blouse-like tops. Freddie dominated the proceedings, of course. Even I was mesmerized by him. It was amazing to see the transformation that came over him with an audience to perform to. It brought something out in him. He was just born to perform. I was also really impressed by the individual talent of all four of them. Roger was a really superb drummer; John held it all together on bass, and Brian, clearly, had the potential to be an outstanding guitarist.

That was the good news. The bad news, however, was the sound was absolutely crap. There was massive feedback coming from the speakers, and I could see that the boys were a bundle of nerves—and that the technical problems were getting to them. Jack and I had advised them to play a few standards in addition to their own material. So as well as stuff like "Keep Yourself Alive" and "Jesus", they did rock 'n' roll numbers like "Johnny B. Good". But as the problems mounted the band grew progressively worse.

Of course, I didn't let on to the invited guests. As far as they were concerned I thought they were the "best thing since sliced bread". But when Dave Thomas came up to me and asked me what I thought, I said, "Eeeuch."

He looked at me as if to say, "I know what the hell we are going to do?"

I looked back and reassured him.

"Don't worry. We can make a band out of this. It's just going to need an awful lot of work."

~

By the end of that year Queen had completed the material for their first album. It sounded great, although of course, the boys soon discovered a few flaws. One track, "Liar", had been overdubbed on to the wrong backing track. A tape operator somewhere in Trident had cocked up.

So we had to devote a bit of extra studio time to sorting out the mess. By the time 1973 arrived, however, it was ready. All we needed now was a record company.

Jack Nelson continued to try to coax and cajole people on both sides of the Atlantic to sign the band and a lot of big labels had turned him down.

Earlier in the year, the annual MIDEM festival came to Cannes. It was the big event on the music calendar. Everyone from the business went there. So we decided to send a team down. We now had four companies to promote, Trident Studios, Trident Audio Developments, Trident Tape Services, and Trident Audio Productions. So we had a crazy idea: instead of paying huge hotel bills, we decided to rent a large motor yacht in Cannes harbour.

Today it's the norm, but back then it was a first, and it upset the management of the event no end, as I understood they were on a percentage of all of the expenditures incurred at the hotels during the festival.

The team comprised myself, Jack Nelson, John Anthony, Peter Robey, my secretary Brit Marie Young, and two models to hand out brochures and look great on our stand, just like a motor show would do things We worked hard—and had a lot of fun too.

Despite the fact it was January and the yacht was supposed to be in the harbour for winter engine maintenance, we decided to throw a lunch one day. Because it was such a novelty to have a yacht, the clamour for tickets was huge.

Somehow I persuaded the captain to let us take the yacht out around the island of L'isle Sainte-Marguerite.

It was a great piece of promotion. There we were flying a Trident flag sailing past the other delegates having their lunch on the Croisette.

It all went swimmingly until John Anthony, Brit, and one of our clients asked to have a run around the bay in the yacht's dingy.

Somehow the boat broke down and they got stuck at sea. We were all so involved with our other lunch guests that we hadn't noticed they were missing.

When they eventually turned up again, we discovered that John Anthony had been forced to drop his trousers and start mooning other boats in order to get noticed.

The Cannes trip proved a really good investment, however.

EMI were at the festival in force, ready to launch a new label. One of their big executives was a guy called Roy Featherstone.

He'd listened to hundreds of tapes that week. "Everything from people's mothers to their howling dogs," he said years later. Then Ronnie Beck handed him the Queen material. We'd put it together along with a mini biography of the boys and the band. The minute Roy put on "Liar" he was hooked.

Ronnie told him that "one or two others" were interested, which gee'd Roy up a bit, even though it was a blatant lie. Soon I was receiving an urgent telegram from the south of France asking me to hold off on signing any major deals until he got back. We had him on the hook.

A couple of things then played in our favour.

Around this time Trident also managed to get Queen a really plum piece of airplay, a slot on Radio 1's hugely influential "Sounds of the Seventies" segment. They went along to the BBC studios in Maida Vale where they played four songs off their new album: "Keep Yourself Alive", "My Fairy King", "Liar", and a song that Brian May had written with Tim Staffell during their Smile days which the boys had reworked in the studio called "Doing Alright".

No sooner had the session been played on Radio 1 in mid-February than EMI were back on the phone trying to insist that they do a deal with Trident for Queen—and Queen only. Again we said no. We felt our bargaining position strengthening by the day.

By the spring of 1973 we'd also begun talking to CBS and their chief executive Clive Davis in the States about them publishing Queen in America and other territories. The music business is a village when it comes down to it. The news that we were talking to CBS forced EMI to cave in and offer us a deal—for all three of our acts.

And so it was that in March 1973 Jack Nelson and I agreed to a label distribution deal for Trident Audio Productions and all three of our artists: Eugene Wallace, Mark Ashton, and Queen—with an option for further artists if we decided to bring them into the Trident stable.

EMI wanted to get the album out as soon as possible and started talking about an autumn release.

Nothing succeeds like success in the entertainment business, and no sooner had news broken that Trident had signed a deal with EMI for the world excluding the Americas and the Far East, then our US deal was coming to fruition. Only it wasn't with CBS.

Our talks with Clive Davis, a notoriously tough negotiator, were dragging. We were going through something like the third draft of a contract the size of the Yellow Pages when an alternative offer suddenly appeared.

Jac Holzman, who ran the respected Elektra label in the States, had been passing through London and met Jack Nelson, an old friend of his. Holzman had heard about Queen and asked to hear them. Jack warned him that he was deep into negotiations with CBS and their formidable boss Clive Davis. Holzman wasn't worried, in fact he'd just beaten Davis to land another artist, the songwriter Harry Chapin.

Jack had handed Holzman a set of acetates containing all the Queen stuff we had. Holzman's reaction was immediate. He said it was "like a perfectly cut diamond landing on your desk." He told Jack that he wanted to do a deal for Queen in the States.

Jack came to tell me all this. I wasn't convinced. CBS were the giants in the States. We were close to landing them. Having said that, their contracts were notoriously unfavourable to artists.

"Let's see what Holzman can come up with," I said.

Holzman's modus operandi was to "love bomb" people he wanted to work with. So suddenly Jack was getting calls from LA, from Tokyo, from everywhere. "I love this band," he kept saying.

Now if it had been someone else, we'd have thought it was bullshit. But Holzman had a solid reputation. He'd established the label himself in the 1950s, at first with a mix of folk, jazz, and gospel artists.

The next time he rang he was in Australia.

As it happened, negotiations with CBS got stuck. We were arguing over some tiny percentage point on royalties or something. So Jack said to Holzman, "Look, come to London and see them play live. I'll put on a gig for you."

We set it up at the Marquee. But, once again, it was a bit of a disaster. The sound wasn't right, and the boys were uptight again. Holzman was deeply disappointed. He said he'd seen nothing on the stage to match the power of the recorded sound. He even wrote a long, four or five page memo, filled with thoughts and suggestions for improving them as a live band. But he didn't give up on the idea of signing them.

A lot of people thought Jack and Trident were mad to go with a relatively small label like Elektra when we'd had CBS on the hook. But Holzman proved as good as his word and would be instrumental in breaking Queen in America—and the wider world.

~

Freddie and the boys were getting very excited about the release of their first album. But, as it turned out, they found themselves being released elsewhere first.

The recording Freddie, Roger, and Brian had done with Robin Cable the previous year had been sitting around the studio gathering dust. But then one day Robin and I decided to listen to it again for some reason.

"This is good, we should stick it out," I said.

We knew we couldn't do anything to jeopardise the launch of Queen, so we couldn't acknowledge that it was their lead singer, guitarist, and drummer on the two tracks.

So we decided to put it out under a pseudonym. The question was what to call him?

The answer popped out one day when someone was talking about another act that was dominating the charts at that time, Gary Glitter.

"We should call him something like Larry Lurex," someone said.

Everyone burst out laughing. We then looked at each other and smiled. Larry Lurex it was.

And so it was that Freddie Mercury, Brian May, and Roger Taylor were first released.

The single didn't do much here in the UK. In fact, it barely sold more than a few hundred copies. (They are all collector's items now, of course.) It made slightly more of a ripple over in the States, where it made No. 115 in the Bubbling Under The Top 100 Chart. Not exactly an earth-shattering success. But that would come soon enough . . .

~

By now we were working closely with EMI on the release of Queen's album. Of course every aspect of the title and cover caused huge arguments in the band.

The title was simply Queen, which we thought worked. But Roger Taylor, for some reason, didn't like it and wanted to call it Top Fax, Pix, and Info instead. No one was keen on that. Another suggestion had been Dearie Me, which was quite funny but seemed to me to draw even more attention to the gay connotation of the band's name. Dearie Me by Queen. The band were a hard enough sell as it was. That was going to make it impossible.

So Queen it was.

They also spent ages arguing about the album sleeve. The front cover was a single image of Freddie on stage, with two spotlights in the background and a purple effect. A pal of Roger Taylor's called Doug Puddifoot took the image, and I think the tinted sepia sort of effect helped the whole image work very well.

For the back cover the boys put together a collage of snaps of themselves. Some had been taken at gigs, but others were of the band posing round at Freddie's flat. Apparently Freddie had driven everyone to distraction fretting over whether he looked "gorgeous enough" in them. They'd eventually enlisted the help of a load of friends to select the best.

The final thing they'd insisted on for the album was a little note that said "no synthesizers were used on this album", or words to that effect. They were conscious of the fact that their heavily produced sound could be misunderstood and that listeners would simply write them off as another synthesizer band. This was a typical example of Queen worrying themselves unnecessarily. Brian, in particular, used to work himself up into a terrible state fretting over whether people "understood" what their music was about and how it was made. We tried to tell him that no one really cared, that they would either like the sound of it or they wouldn't, but it didn't stop him worrying. As it happened, the release of the album and first single didn't do much to ease his nerves. Well, at first anyway.

In advance of the album coming out on July 13th, we'd decided to put "Keep Yourself Alive" out as the first single a week or so beforehand. The reviews were pretty good. Record Mirror called it "a raucous, well built single". Intriguingly the NME said "if these guys look half as good as they sound they could be huge". But one or two others weren't so keen. Melody Maker said it "lacks originality" and Sounds felt it "never really gets going". More worryingly, Radio 1 rejected it for their all-important play list. They did it not just once, but five times. There was nothing we could do to persuade them. Only Alan Freeman played it on the BBC, although we did also get some decent airplay from Radio Luxembourg. The situation was soon improving, however.

Fortunately, someone had had the good sense to send a white label copy of the album to the producer of the Old Grey Whistle Test, Mike Appleton. Unfortunately, he or she forgot to put any information in there about what the record was or who it was by. All it had on the white label was "Keep Yourself Alive". It actually proved to be an accidental masterstroke.

Mike Appleton got the record and was intrigued. He stuck it on the turntable and loved it. He immediately decided to play "Keep Yourself Alive" on the next edition of Whistle Test, along with one of the slightly wacky films that was the show's trademark at the time. The film he chose was a piece of animation that had apparently once been used by US President Roosevelt as part of his election campaign. Surreal.

When it went out the impact was huge. Whistle Test had the power to make a band overnight, and it certainly felt like they'd just done it for us. The BBC fielded loads of calls about the music, including one from Trident confirming that the track was by one of our own bands.

It worked a treat, it wasn't long before John Peel, the most influential DJ on Radio 1, was on the phone asking whether they would do a session for him. We'd seen the effect "Sound of the Seventies" had had and knew John Peel carried even more weight. So we jumped at it. They headed into the BBC studio and recorded a session playing "Keep Yourself Alive", "Liar", and "Son and Daughter" from the new album along with a new, unpublished track called "See What A Fool I've Been".

As I listened to the session broadcast in my office late one night a week or so later, I couldn't help taking stock of things—not just with Queen but with Trident as a whole.

~

To say 1973 had been a good year for Trident and me would be a massive understatement. Our daughter Samantha had been born in February—we were now a family of six!—and that year we swept the board at the biggest music industry awards, the Music Week Awards held at the Hilton Hotel on Park Lane. Trident won Top Studio, Ken Scott won Best Engineer, and we were runners up to Apple for top Disc Cutting and Mastering. Awards, as if that wasn't testimony enough to our dominance, virtually all the artists who were up there collecting awards were people who had recorded with us. David Bowie won two big awards for top male and best album. Carly Simon, who'd recorded "You're So Vain" with us, also picked up a big award. We nearly drank the place dry of champagne that night too, I can tell you.

The success meant that we were now in a position to expand into new and exciting areas. The music business was changing fast, and I sensed that the next big thing was going to be video, which fascinated me. With this in mind, we'd purchased Lion Television, a video subsidiary of British Lion Films based at Shepperton film studios. The deal had come about in a pretty complicated way.

We had actually looked at buying this company about a year earlier, but the owners had wanted a ridiculous amount for it. Time had gone by, however, and the whole Shepperton complex had been purchased by a company called Vavasseur, which was run by John Bentley. It turned out that he'd also just purchased a major toy manufacturer and was having a lot of trouble with the trade unions over redundancies. He was planning to redevelop part of Shepperton and was concerned he would run into more union problems, so he approached me after finding our names on previous correspondences.

The deal they proposed to me was that, on condition that we take over Lion Television lock, stock, and barrel—including the twelve staff members—within thirty days, they would reduce the original asking price by about forty percent. It was simply too good to miss, but we didn't have that sort of money available at that time, so I took a chance.

I suggested that we would take over the business immediately, but that they would pay the first month's salaries and we would pay for the business in stage payments. I was astounded when they said yes, although it was a decision I would later regret.

Ideally we would have called the new company Trident Television, but someone else had taken the name. So I combined Trident with Lion and came up with Trilion—which still meant three.

The other big step we'd made by now had been to move into the music console market. A year or so back, we'd decided that we needed a new recording console for the studio. The only problem was that no manufacturer had been able to deliver what we wanted.

Malcolm Toft, who had by now moved up to become studio manager, had suggested to Barry and me that he thought he could build a desk that met all of the things our engineering team wanted. We agreed that he and our maintenance engineer Barry Porter should build a small desk for our copy room as a demo unit.

It turned out to be an excellent piece of kit, so Barry and I decided to give Malcolm a budget and some space to try and build a full-scale version. All of the engineers at Trident contributed with their input.

So when Malcolm finished the first "A Range" console, it was truly built and "designed by engineers for engineers".

We had a minor hiccup when it was finished. Having built the console to fit the size of the building, Malcolm suddenly realised that the desk, which he'd been building on the top floor, couldn't travel down to the studio a couple of floors below it.

I'd initially laughed at him.

"Don't be stupid. I built this place and I know the door sizes," I'd said. But when I measured up I realised the top floor was narrower than the bottom. Our in-house carpenter Bernie had to take down the doorframe and part of the wall. That took a while for me to live down, but I didn't much care. The Trident "A Range" quickly became one of the most admired and sought-after pieces of equipment in the music industry.

In anticipation of the expansion that was about to take place, we'd already started spreading out from St. Anne's Court. With the music side of things taking over the studio, we'd got an office for the admin side of things over on Wardour Street. If we got our business up and running as I planned, then I had my eye on a building on the corner of Brewer Street that would be an ideal headquarters for all of the Trident Companies. There was a hell of a lot going on.

At that point, however, I had a real feeling that the most exciting thing that we had on our hands might just be Queen.

They were far from home and dry. In fact, they'd got nowhere yet. But it felt like we'd made a start. It felt like they were up and running.

Of course it was still a huge financial gamble, one which—as things stood—I was going to lose. The advance we'd had from EMI was just £4,000 (c.£40,000). We were due to get another £7,000 for their second album when that was finished, but that was a while off. Even when it came in that wouldn't recoup what we'd spent.

"Have I been foolish?" I said once more to myself as I sat in my office listening to the John Peel show. Those words would actually prove to be more prophetic than I could have possibly imagined.

1972

1974

TRIDENT

46 Track is at home with Trident
-direct to disc too
Contact: 01-734 9901/3 and get into the picture

1974

1972 (p.156-157) **LEFT PAGE:** *Full page:* Elton John at the mixing desk in Trident's first remix room.
RIGHT PAGE: (clockwise) *Top:* Genisis in session. *Middle right:* John Anthony listening to a play back. *Bottom right:* Elton John 'Rocket Man' sleeve. *Bottom left:* Elton John. *Middle left:* Carly Simon with Robin Cable, during the making of the 'No Secrets' album.

1974 (p.158-159) **LEFT PAGE:** (clockwise) *Top:* Trident's Control room. *Middle right:* The disc cutting suite. *Bottom right:* The orange Trident mastering sleeve. *Bottom left:* The Studio. *Middle left:* The new re-mix room.
RIGHT PAGE: *Full page:* Gentle Giant in session at Trident.

1974 (p.160-161) **LEFT PAGE:** *Full Page:* Advertising poster illustrating the many facets of Trident's services within a single group of Companies.
RIGHT PAGE: *Top:* Studio showing the 'famous' Beckstein piano used by Beatles, Elton John, Queen and David Bowie etc

1978 (p.162-163) **LEFT PAGE:** (clockwise) T*op:* Trilion filming Thin Lizzy's 'Do Anything You Want To' music video at the Brewer st. studio. *Bottom right:* Trilion filming the first Papal visit of Pope John Paul II at Dublin Airport 1979. *Bottom left:* Leo Sayer on a crane filming a promo outside Trilion's Soho offices.
RIGHT PAGE: (clockwise) *Top:* The World famous Trident 'A Range' desk. *Middle right: Trilion Video outside broadcast trucks showing their new Trilion livery. Lower Middle right:* The completed Capital Radio London broadcast truck built by Norman and his team as a special project. *Bottom right:* Trident Tape Services factory duplication room.
Bottom left: Trilion edit suite where the Queen's 'Bohemian Rhapsody' music video was edited –regarded as the first ever music video. Middle bottom left: The Brewer St. Studio. *Middle left:* Norman talking to some of the Trilion crew.

197

Nine

Hitting The Road

"He introduced them as "stuck up Pommies" and mooned to the audience to signal his contempt for the visitors."

By August of 1973 the music video side of the business was well and truly up and running. Trilion Video were based at Shepperton film studios. It was the natural choice to shoot with Trilion when Jack Nelson and I decided to make a promotional film to send to the US, where Elektra were revving up to release Queen's first album.

It was an eventful shoot. At first the mood had been good. Freddie arrived announcing to everyone that he'd shaved his chest for the proceedings. He spent what felt like an eternity with the make up girls, getting ready for his "close-up". But the nerves soon started to set in by the time they went on to the set so the boys were quite edgy.

The director I had hired was Mike Mansfield, with whom I had worked years earlier on a TV show called "The Tale of Two Rivers" with the band "Unit Four Plus Two". Mike had painted the whole stage a bright white and the minute the boys saw it they started to have their doubts. They were wearing black and white outfits and the effect really didn't work. Despite this, we ploughed on. We were using our own staff, so we weren't going to waste them.

Queen were performing to playback tapes of two of their tracks, "Liar" and "Keep Yourself Alive". But at this stage in their careers miming like this was alien to them, and it took a load of takes to get it right. Even then, the white background didn't look right. We'd later have to re-shoot it with smoke effects and darker lighting. The second version was directed by another old friend of mine and ex-fellow musician who was a TV Director, working at London Weekend - Bruce Gowers who we knew as Gus Gowers

The film was all part of a concerted effort to take Queen up to the next level. As part of this we'd hired one of London's top publicists, Tony Brainsby. Brainsby, a tall, bespectacled character who drove around in a Rolls, had the Midas touch when it came to generating publicity for rock acts. He'd worked with Paul McCartney and his new band Wings, The Strawbs, Mott the Hoople, and many others.

He'd found Queen a bit of a publicist's dream. At his first meeting with them Freddie had laid out his entire master plan. He'd given Tony photos, a copy of his logo, and all sorts of ideas.

He didn't agree with all of them but he was soon setting the wheels in motion for interviews and features on the band. The film was going to be an extra string to our bow.

By now Queen were back in the studio to start work on their second album. For the first time, however, they were now a fully fledged recording band and were booked into the studio the same way as every other act. Once more Freddie and Brian had started experimenting with all sorts of sounds and effects. In a way, they'd been spoilt by having so much free time in the past. You couldn't get them out of there sometimes.

Things were still building slowly for Queen. The main buzz was happening out in the States where Elektra were ready to release the first album. It quickly got airplay and plenty of fan requests soon after. In contrast to the UK, where the album hadn't made a dent on the charts, it hit the all-important Billboard chart in the US within a few weeks of its release, reaching a respectable No. 83. For a new, unheard British band it was quite an achievement. It confirmed my feeling that we were on to something potentially very big.

As it stood, however, until and unless we could get the band established, Queen were nothing more than a big expense for Trident. That autumn, for instance, the BBC asked to film them for their In Concert series and arranged a gig for the Golders Green Hippodrome.

The boys used it to try out a track from their new album called "Procession". It went down well, which they were pleased about because it was an ambitious piece. The whole show went down a storm.

Afterwards Jack and I agreed that we had to get them ready for the next step now: a live tour.

We'd been holding back on this until now for several reasons. First of all, they'd not been the greatest live band I'd ever seen. It was more of a technical issue than anything else. The boys could play, we knew that. But the show didn't do justice to their sound. I'd seen that firsthand at The Pheasantry gig.

The other issue was that we had to introduce them as a live act at the right level.

Queen weren't a band that were going to work in the sort of twenty-pound-a-night pubs and clubs that bands traditionally played in when they were trying to make it. Their music was too challenging and complex for that. There was also an element of showmanship to their act, especially Freddie. We didn't want to dilute or diminish that in any way by putting on a cheap stage show.

Just as we'd been careful to build the band up slowly in the studio, we had to do the same thing with their live performances. We wanted them to play in big venues with decent lighting and sound systems.

Jack's contacts book was as good as anyone's. He knew everybody. Pretty soon he'd started talking to a guy called Bob Hirschmann, who managed Mott the Hoople. They'd recorded at Trident with David Bowie producing, and were doing pretty well with one of Bowie's songs called "All The Young Dudes". They were booked on a decent-sized tour that was going to take in some of the country's best venues.

Bob was sceptical at first, but Jack was a good salesman. And we sweetened the deal for Bob by offering him a three thousand pound advance for the hire of the Mott's PA system. By the end of the year they were on the road with them.

To ensure that we launched them correctly, we decided to step up our investment even more. We hired two top guys to oversee their sound and lighting: John Harris, an old friend of the band, did the sound, while James Dann, Elton John's lighting director, did the lighting. In the run-up to the tour we kept them on weekly retainers so that they could make sure the show was perfect from the very first gig. We'd also set up some publicity in Europe, including a couple of live performances in Frankfurt and Luxembourg. The latter was a disaster. We'd arranged for the band to play Radio Luxembourg and put the performance out as an In Concert special. But the technical side was all up the creek and they ended up without a proper recording of it. Back in England, they organised one final warm-up gig at Imperial College, where they'd played a lot of their earliest gigs and where their fan base was extremely solid.

Of course, none of this came cheap. And nor did all the extra equipment we were already forking out as the tour took shape. There were times when I opened the Queen accounts and sat there shaking my head in disbelief. This was one such occasion.

~

The Mott the Hoople tour kicked off in mid-November, 1973. As Queen hit the road for the first time, the creative tension within the band was still as high as ever.

It was clear that they were nervous. When they took to the stage at their first gig at Leeds Town Hall, the normally effervescent Freddie was subdued. He spoke softly introducing each song and didn't try and get any rapport going with the crowd, which was not his style at all.

There were technical troubles too, and they'd often blow a fuse— literally. After one gig, Roger kicked his drum kit across the stage and Brian chucked his precious guitar down so violently he almost smashed it.

Just like in the studio, it would all calm down immediately afterwards.

The boys weren't heavy drinkers or anything like that. But they did like to party after a show. They'd go for a big meal with loads of friends or hang out in their hotel until the small hours.

They were also heavily into taking vitamin pills. They used to pop them like they were sweets. They reckoned they replaced all the salt they were losing when they were on stage.

It was clear though that they were winning fans—and lots of them.

I went along to the final gig in London, at the Hammersmith Odeon, and was amazed at the turnout. There were even grandparents turning up with their grandchildren. It was clear they were appealing to people right across the generations.

Among the older generation in the audience when they played Hammersmith were Brian's parents, who were seeing their son play live for the first time in their lives. Some fans rumbled who they were and asked them for their autographs, which made their night I think.

By the end of the tour, it was pretty clear to everyone who saw the gig that there were as many people there for Queen as were there for Mott. Queen were getting more encores and bigger cheers than the supposed headliners. Of course, this didn't go down too well with Ian Hunter, a volatile character at the best of times. And he didn't hold back from making his feelings plain.

To mark the end of the tour at the Hammersmith Odeon we threw a party in the upper balcony area. We invited a load of people, including, for some reason that escapes me now, Andy Williams, the American crooner. He was huge at the time.

We had this big cake marking the end of the tour, and a few people were giving speeches. Bob Hirschmann praised Mott and their crew, saying what a great job they'd done. There were cheers and applause, but when he did the same for Queen, there was even more of a reception. It was all too much for Ian Hunter to take.

Before anyone knew what was going on, he just stepped forward and punched his fist into the cake. The mess it made was unbelievable. Bits of sponge and cream and jam and stuff went flying everywhere including all over Andy William's suit!!

A lot of people were shocked and didn't know what to say. But most of us just thought it was hilarious. Freddie was pissing himself with laughter. He thought it was the funniest thing he'd ever seen. And, of course, he loved the fact that Ian Hunter was jealous of the reception he and his band had been getting.

There was no doubt though that Queen had persuaded the sceptical Bob Hirschmann of their value. Sure enough, he was soon inviting them to accompany Mott on a tour of America in the following year. The minute I heard it I felt two things: excitement at the prospect of cracking America, the band were really starting to show the true colours, their show was great, and a knot in my stomach about the extra expense it was going to involve.

~

Before they hit America, however, Queen had to make the long trip down to Australia to honour a promise they had made, to play there in the New Year.

They were due to fly out at the end of January 1974 and spent the Christmas and New Year holidays recovering from their tour and having the injections they needed to travel Down Under.

I'd always had the feeling the boys weren't as physically strong as they needed to be, particularly Brian and Freddie. For all the vitamins they took, they seemed undernourished and frail. I worried for them. My suspicions proved to be right when Brian suddenly developed a really high fever a couple of weeks before they were due to fly to Australia. The doctors diagnosed a fever which they guessed had been caused by the injections. As if to prove it, his arm had swollen up to the size of a football.

It wasn't that simple, however. The doctors gave Brian medicine to treat an infection, but it didn't help. In fact the problem got even worse. The boys were intelligent and had a grasp of medicine. They could tell it was something serious and they pressed the doctors to run more tests. Eventually they diagnosed gangrene.

With Brian in the hospital, the others were thrown into a complete panic. It threw me as well.

Just as things seemed to be falling into place, this was happening.

Jack kept me and the rest of the team up to date with what was going on and for a while the noises coming from the hospital were ominous. Jack told me that, at one point, it had been touch and go whether Brian would lose his arm. If he had, of course, that would have been the end of Queen there and then. But luckily the crisis eased off and he was allowed to leave the hospital—and to fly to Australia.

Mind you, he probably wished he hadn't when he got there.

Queen already had a bit of a love-hate relationship with the press in the UK. Freddie, in particular, was quite happy to antagonise journalists, some of whom were already writing bitchy, sniping pieces about his camp personality.

The nastiness of the British press paled into insignificance when they got to Oz, however. I was back in London, but there were telexes and phone calls flooding back into the Trident offices at such a rate I might as well have been there. Every day, it seemed, there was a new problem to deal with.

It was actually Jack and Trident's fault as much as Queen's. We'd booked them to headline a festival in a place called Sunbury. This immediately got up the noses of the Aussie bands who wanted to know how an unknown English band had got themselves top of the bill. If it had been Led Zeppelin, maybe they'd have understood, but Queen? Who the fuck were they? And who the fuck did they think they were?

As if to make matters worse, we'd sent Queen's own lighting rig over to them—at huge expense once more of course. The rig was so complicated it also needed a home-grown crew to operate it, which again got the locals' backs up—and understandably so. What was so special about this British lighting rig that an Aussie couldn't operate it?

The icing on the cake was the boys' over-the-top behaviour. They arrived in Sydney as if they really were Led Zeppelin or The Rolling Stones, being swept around in white limousines and behaving like royalty. The local press had taken against them almost immediately. For a start, a band called Queen was a bit of a red rag to the republican, anti-Royalist wing of the press. A lot of the papers wrote pieces taking the piss out of them and slagging off their attitude. Tony Brainsby did his best to get some friendly journos on our side but, to be honest, I wasn't too concerned about that. Sometimes bad publicity is worth more than good. More worrying for me and Jack was the boys' health.

They hadn't travelled well. Brian hadn't fully recovered from his gangrene scare and, as if that wasn't bad enough, Freddie had picked up an ear infection. They spent a large part of their first few days in Oz holed up in their hotel rooms, popping pills and sleeping.

They were still a bit under par when it came to the concert.

Freddie and Brian wanted to make maximum use of their light show and kept the audience waiting until the sun had gone down before coming on stage. With a load of beers inside them, the locals had taken exception to this and started slow hand-clapping them.

The local DJ who was introducing them had clearly taken against them as well, because when he arrived on stage he introduced them as "stuck up Pommies" and mooned to the audience to signal his contempt for the visitors.

When the boys got on stage it apparently got even worse. Someone had deliberately sabotaged the lighting rig, and the sound was also wrong. Freddie couldn't hear himself singing. On top of all this Brian's arm was killing him, which meant his performance was under par as well.

From what Jack and the others told me afterwards, the concert had actually been pretty good. But the crowd had turned against them and that was that. The whole sorry event came to an end when the DJ cut short their encore by asking the crowd whether they'd rather hear more of "those Pommy bastards" or a "good old Aussie band" instead. Naturally, the crowd had gone for the latter.

The press laid into them the next day and the whole thing turned into a bit of a diplomatic incident. The boys were mightily relieved when they got on a plane back to London, although there was one final twist to their touring nightmare.

For some bizarre reason, the British press had been tipped off that Her Majesty The Queen was arriving at Heathrow. So when they saw four knackered musicians emerging through customs, they weren't too happy. The band were making enemies all over the world, or so it seemed to them anyway.

~

The reality was very different, however. By the time they got back from Oz, the band was able to admire its second album, which was completed and ready for release. A single, "Seven Seas of Rhye", was ready to go out as well, backed by a top EMI promotions guy called Ronnie Fowler and Radio plugger Eric Hall, later to become a football agent. They told us that they were determined to break Queen into the big league—and they were as good as their word.

Ronnie spent the first weeks of February 1974 coaxing and cajoling every influential music industry person in London. He was begging, calling in favours, trying everything he could think to get people to take notice of Queen. His persistence paid off.

One evening, Ronnie got a phone call from a frazzled producer at Top of the Pops. An act that was supposed to be appearing on that week's show had pulled out. He needed a replacement. "Got anyone?" he asked.

At the time Ronnie was promoting two bands, Queen and a London act featuring Steve Harley and Cockney Rebel. He suggested that Top of the Pops take Queen, something Steve Harley was furious about.

It proved the turning point.

Top of the Pops still insisted that all acts mime to a backing track, so Queen had to record the track that same night. Unfortunately Trident was full, so we had to squeeze them in elsewhere in town. The next day they rushed over to the BBC's Ramport Studios, where Top of the Pops was filmed, and shot their performance. It went out the following evening on February 21, 1974.

The boys watched it on a TV in the window of an electrical shop, apparently.

Queen really connected with the performance. All the personality, power, and creativity that I'd seen years earlier was there on the TV screen. They looked different—and they looked great.

Of course, they were also a pain in the proverbial ass too. Such was the reaction to the performance that we had to rush out a white label pressing of "Seven Seas of Rhye" at the speed of sound. Radio 1 had agreed to play the single extensively, almost guaranteeing that it would be a hit.

We were all cracking open a bottle when Freddie was on the phone demanding that we send them a different version. He'd listened to the white label mix and spotted that it was the wrong pressing. So we had to work overnight to get new ones done and over to Radio

1 before daybreak. We could all happily have strangled Freddie for that, except, of course, he was right.

Sure enough, the combination of Top of the Pops and wall-to-wall Radio 1 airplay did the trick—as it always did. The reviews were great. New Musical Express said "this single showcases all their power and drive, their writing talents, and every quality that makes them unique." That went down well, I can tell you.

Even better, the single went into the charts, entering at No. 45 in the first week of March. It was the boys' first hit and they were completely chuffed about it. A couple of days later, their album Queen II came out, also entering the chart, eventually reaching No. 35.

One or two people were sniffy about it. Record Mirror called it "the dregs of glam rock". But, generally, the reviews were very good. It marked a really significant turning point in their story.

Until this point, Freddie had continued to maintain his interest in his stall at Kensington Market, which he ran with his girlfriend Mary Austin. Brian too, had continued to work, at one point teaching English. He'd also carried on working on his thesis. John had taken things even further and started an MSc course. But the success of the single and Queen II changed all that.

Until that point, no matter what they said publicly, deep down I don't think any of them had quite believed it was going to happen. From then on, however, that all changed. Suddenly they started to really believe they were going to be stars. And they really started behaving like it too.

It wasn't a luxury all of us could afford, however. We still had businesses to run that was funding Queen.

Ten

Mr Big

" People often asked me whether I had to pay any protection money during all my years working in the middle of Soho. The honest answer was no. Not a penny. Mind you, it wasn't for the want of trying in some cases. "

One morning, early in 1974, I got a call from the receptionist at my new office, across the road from the studio.

"Norman, there's someone on his way up to see you," she said.

"Who is it?"

"Don Arden," she said, dropping her voice to a whisper. "He's got a couple of heavies with him."

"All right," I said, drawing on a cigarette. "I've got a good idea what this is all about."

He revelled in nicknames like "Mr. Big", "The British Godfather", and the "English Al Capone".

There were all sorts of stories in circulation about Don, some of them myths I was pretty sure. One that was pretty much agreed to be true concerned him and the impresario Robert Stigwood. Apparently Stigwood had made some sort of approach to manage Don's then star act, The Small Faces. Don and a gang of heavies had marched into Stigwood's office and threatened to hang him out of a window if he tried to poach any of his acts again. There were other stories about him threatening his acts if they ever challenged his "accounting methods". A lot of people were terrified by him, but I wasn't one of them.

I was pretty certain he was not making a social call. He and I had just had a run in—over money.

One of the acts Don was involved with had done some recording at Trident. The trouble was the bill remained unpaid. It was quite a big bill, a few thousand quid if my memory serves me correct. So I was sitting on the masters until he coughed up.

I knew that Don wanted to release the masters to CBS, who were going to release the album. I knew this because CBS had also been on the phone to me chasing up the masters. It was holding up the production schedules and was getting quite serious. I'd told them that they couldn't have them because of unpaid bills. I said I was going to hold them in escrow, or lien, until I got my money.

This hadn't gone down well with Don, who'd been on the phone to me immediately. We'd had what you might call a forthright exchange. He'd called me every name under the sun and I'd given as good as I'd got. The air had been pretty blue.

So I knew what was coming now. He was going to try a little less gentle persuasion.

A few moments after I put down the phone, the door burst open and in walked the short, stocky figure of Don. He was living up to the Al Capone image, draped in a suit and dangling a cigar from his mouth. I couldn't help smiling inwardly. I don't know what had happened to him, but he was also carrying a walking stick. Looking down I saw that he had one leg in plaster.

"Where are my fucking masters?" he demanded.

I played it cool.

"Hello Don, nice to see you, have you come round with a cheque?"

"No, I fucking haven't," he growled.

"I told you Don," I said. "I'm holding them in lien until you pay. No cheque, no masters."

Don was a bully, nothing more nothing less. He didn't like being told no. So he walked, well actually hobbled, close enough to me to be able to bang his walking stick on my desk. Wham.

"I want my fucking masters and I want them now," he said, by now looking pretty red in the face.

I wasn't going to be intimidated. "Do that again Don, and I'll break that stick over your back," I said. "By the way you've only got one leg to stand on so it's going to be easy isn't it?"

He'd come in on his own, but the noise had drawn his two gorillas into the room.

"Who are these? Tweedledum and Tweedledee?" I said.

I then picked up the phone and dialled my brother Barry over in the studio.

"Barry, Don Arden's over here with a couple of his gorillas. I think they want to have a party. Can you bring all the lads over," I said putting down the phone.

Don was standing there, steam coming out of his ears.

"Right, I've got twenty-two blokes coming over. Fancy your chances?

I knew full well that Don was all mouth and trousers. He wasn't going to do anything.

Sure enough, he just whacked a chair with his walking stick, turned, and started shuffling out.

"I'll have you later," he said, turning round in one final act of defiance.

"Yeah, yeah, Don," I said. "How are you going to do that standing on one leg?"

I couldn't help but laugh.

Of course, the world was full of characters like Don. It was just that Soho seemed to have more than it's fair share of them than anywhere else.

People often asked me whether I had to pay any protection money during all my years working in the middle of Soho. The honest answer was no. Not a penny. Mind you, it wasn't for the want of trying in some cases.

One afternoon the receptionist at the Brewer Street offices called up to me and said I had another unannounced guest.

"There's a policeman here to see you," she said.

"Show him up," I said, mildly curious to see who it was.

This guy came into my office and whacked his warrant card out on to the desk.

"I understand you owe a couple of restaurants in Soho a few hundred quid," he said.

"Quite likely," I said, shrugging my shoulders, we have many accounts around here and half the blokes in the offices spend their lives in restaurants negotiating deals with clients"

"Well, I've come to collect the money," he said.

"Oh right, so you're a debt collector," I said.

He just looked at me and sneered.

"No. A debt advisory service," he said.

"Oh, I see. We'll get you a cup of tea and get something organised," I said.

A friend of mine was a member of the CID at Savile Row. His mates used to come round on some Friday afternoons when they were off duty with a bottle of scotch and sit in my boardroom and watch movies on link up. We had a satellite link direct with the post office tower, so you could watch anything you wanted. Anything. It was all hardwired satellite. They'd sit there all afternoon drinking and playing cards. I didn't mind. It made me feel safe. After leaving this copper in my office, I got straight on the phone to Saville Row and asked for my mate.

I told him what was going on.

"Really," he said. "Keep him there with a cup of tea."

"No problem," I said.

Savile Row police station was only a few hundred yards away.

By the time I'd organised a cup of tea and got back to my office, my mate from CID was already on his way up. By the time I'd given the guy his tea and sat down again, he was bursting in through the door.

"Who the fuck are you and what are you doing here?" he said, cutting straight to the chase.

The other guy gave him a cocky look and produced his warrant card.

"I'd be careful if I was you. I'm a copper," he said.

My mate produced his card and said, "So am I, and I out-rank you. What are you doing on my patch?"

This guy was out the door, like a rocket. His arse never touched the ground.

People ask me time and time again if I ever get asked for protection money. I always say the same thing, not a thing, didn't need to. Not with friends like that. The restaurant got paid in the normal way.

~

Of course, thanks to people like Don Arden, the music business had a reputation for being a bit dodgy back then. I'd known from my earliest days with The Hunters that there were crooks—bandidos, as I called them. Don Arden himself had admitted that he'd broken The Small Faces into the charts in the mid-sixties by spending £12,000 (c.£120,000) on what he called "chart fixing". Payola wasn't quite as rife as it used to be, but there were still dodgy deals going down all the time. Radio stations and promotion people still had a slightly murky, mysterious relationship.

It was that sort of business. There was a lot of money flying around, and money causes problems. Inevitably, we'd had one or two problems along those lines at Trident.

In February that year, for instance, Ken Scott had produced a new band called Supertramp. They'd had a couple of albums but were on the cusp of breaking through with their third album, Crime of the Century.

Perhaps it was the title of the album, but Ken got it into his head that there was something dodgy going on in our business arrangements with him.

It all ended up with him storming into my office. He then marched out with the gold record for George Harrison's All Things Must Pass album.

I was pretty steamed up about it, I must admit. I remember running into a meeting room, which was the only place with a window out into the street below. It was from there that Ken heard me shouting the immortal lines "you'll never work in this fucking town again!"

Of course he would—and he did. With us, and Ken and I are still friends to this day

No matter where you went in the music business, there were arguments about money. Queen were no different. Even at the beginning, before they were signed they were on a decent wage plus expenses. But that wasn't nearly enough to furnish Freddie's lavish lifestyle even back then, it seemed. He was constantly trying to extract more money out of us.

"What's it for?" I'd ask him.

"Costumes dearie," he'd say.

"I thought you had some," I'd say.

"You don't understand Norman" he'd say with a flick of the wrist. I'd always give in. I knew Queen would come good for us at some point, barring any unforeseen circumstances. Unfortunately, with Queen, there were always plenty of those . . .

~

Queen had headed off to America for their tour with Mott the Hoople feeling on top of the world. They were really fired up, and left the UK with ambitions to conquer the States in one fell swoop by criss-crossing the country.

It all started off well enough, even though they were playing in venues that didn't always fit Freddie's idea of where he should be playing. Jack told me about one place they played, the Harrisburg Farm Arena, where they appeared in May. The place was basically a giant cowshed. It had been cleared out only days before the concert and still bore that telltale smell. Freddie had taken one whiff of it and nearly passed out. Almost as offensive to him was the billing at that gig. Queen were appearing with another up and coming act called Aerosmith. Come the day of the concert, no one could agree on which band would go on before Mott the Hoople, the unquestioned headliners.

It had, of course, led to arguments. Brian May got so fed up with it that he and a member of Aerosmith, Joe Perry, had slid off and drunk a bottle of Jack Daniels. By the time the argument had finally come to a close, Brian and Joe were legless. He admitted later that he'd not been able to hear a thing on stage and had compensated by being a lot more animated than usual. The crowd loved it, but Brian made a pledge afterwards.

It was the first—and last—time Brian ever played a gig drunk. But from then on, he became much more animated on stage.

I don't think it had anything to do with the Jack Daniels, but Brian's health was soon deteriorating. Some of us weren't sure whether he'd ever shaken off the effects of his gangrene earlier in the year.

Sure enough, when they arrived in New York to play the Uris

Theatre on Broadway, he started feeling unwell again. They'd sold out six nights at the venue and made it through them all. But the night after the final gig, Brian collapsed. He travelled to Boston where they were due to play next, but was confined to bed in his hotel while doctors ran tests.

Our worst fears were confirmed when the doctors announced that he had hepatitis. It meant that not only the Boston gig, but the rest of the US tour would have to be cancelled. In addition, Freddie, John, and Roger—as well as every member of the crew and everyone they'd come into contact with during their tour—would all have to be tested for hepatitis. It was, not to put too fine a point on it, a disaster, both personally and professionally.

We arranged for Brian to be given the finest medical treatment and flown back to the UK within hours, as Hepatitis means quarantine in the US. But the band's hopes of cracking America were dashed. Elektra released "Seven Seas of Rhye" in May, but it didn't make an impression.

~

Brian remained confined to quarters throughout most of the summer. As he did so, the rest of the band started work on some new songs for a third album. By July he was well enough to join them at the Rockfield studios down in Wales, where they started laying down tracks.

But Brian was clearly not right. When they came back to London to start recording with us at Trident in August, he was taken seriously ill again.

This time we rushed him to King's College Hospital. As before, everyone at Trident was extremely anxious about him. He had to have an emergency operation for a duodenal ulcer. His recurring illness meant that the plans for a return to the US in September that year had to be scrapped.

Brian felt he'd let the band down. But what could he do? In his absence, Roy Thomas Baker, who was producing the third album (by now called Sheer Heart Attack), had taken an increasingly important role. So much so in fact that Barry and I had christened him the fifth Queenie.

Brian was out of the woods by September 1974. He was even well enough to attend a presentation at the Café Royal to mark the first hundred thousand sales of Queen II. With typical imagination, Tony Brainsby came up with the idea of getting the well-known impersonator Jeanette Charles to play Queen Elizabeth II. She handed the silver disc over to the boys, who—of course—lapped up the media attention.

That was nothing compared to what was to come, however.

On October 11th, EMI put out Queen's third single, "Killer Queen", the lead single from the new album. It was clearly the best thing the boys had done so far.

This time, we didn't need any lucky breaks to get on Top of the Pops or on Radio 1. It was played to death from the moment it came out. Within weeks it had given the boys the thing they'd most wanted —a No. 1 single—as it reached the top in the newspaper charts and No. 2 in the official BBC chart. It was the perfect tonic for Brian, and it gave the band the lift they needed. We were soon planning a series of new gigs, in the UK this time, investing in yet more lighting, pyrotechnics, and sound equipment. We even began planning a movie based on the band playing live, something that no one had attempted yet.

It fits in perfectly with the way we all now saw the band going. As Freddie said repeatedly at the time, he wanted the next twelve months to be the band's biggest and the best. "I want it to be a real show," he kept announcing.

The next year would certainly be that.

Eleven

Freddiepoos

"The organisers had hired a group of giant Sumo wrestlers to control the growing crowds, but even they were soon struggling."

As Queen hit the road again, this time as a headline act in their own right, it was clear that they were on the verge of major league success. "Killer Queen" had become a huge hit not just in the UK, but globally as well. To no one's surprise, tickets for the gigs that promoter Mel Bush put together quickly sold out. Unfortunately, we were still in a situation where the costs were greater than the returns.

That was hardly surprising, given the scale and ambition of this latest tour. Freddie had lived up to his promise and was determined to deliver a real show.

We'd splashed out on yet another new lighting rig and had added a whole host of pyrotechnic effects. There were smoke guns and dry ice machines, fireworks—you name it, we had it. To transport it all around we'd invested in a huge truck and an expanded team of roadies. It was a huge operation, and the costs to Trident were eye watering. There was no question it was going to pay off further down the road. But that road seemed to be stretching ever further into the distance.

The tour kicked off at the Palace Theatre in Manchester at the end of October and was a hit from the start. The boys had developed the act—and added some nice touches to their big rock numbers as well. In one number, "Bring Back Leroy Brown", John Deacon played a single note on a triangle while Brian played a ukulele and Freddie sat around drinking champagne. Then, at the end of the show, they'd recorded a special version of the National Anthem, "God Save the Queen". The fans again loved it.

There was no doubt that Freddie was the star of the show. He would strut around commanding the stage, whipping the crowd up into a frenzy. They adored him, there was no question. The more adulation he received on stage, however, the harder he became to work with off stage.

He was incredibly talented, but he lived life by his rules. He really was a law unto himself. It was making life difficult for the rest of the band—and indeed everyone else who had to work with him, myself included.

The smallest little things could set him off, especially when it concerned his appearance. Freddie was becoming more and more pernickety about what he wore. During the sound check for one concert during their tour that year, he lost a silver snake bracelet. It flew off his wrist as he was singing. Well everything had to stop while we searched for that bracelet. He couldn't go on singing without it on. It didn't matter to him that we were wasting time crawling around on our hands and knees looking for it. Everything and everyone had to be put on hold until Freddie found his precious bloody bracelet.

I had come to realise that Freddie lived for attention and excitement. On stage, he could get as much of it as he wanted. Indeed, there were times when he got too much.

He loved interacting with the crowd and had developed this habit of going right up to the front of the stage so that he could touch the fans. They were encouraging this by throwing gifts and knick-knacks on to the stage. They'd lob everything on there—rings and bracelets, cushions, and dolls. In an interview, Brian had said he liked penguins. So some of them had started chucking little stuffed penguins on to the stage. Freddie lapped it all up of course.

Dave Thomas and the bouncers who were running the tour's security operation had warned him about this.

"Freddie, you're going to come unstuck one night," they'd told him. But he'd just waved them away with one of those regal flicks of his wrist and told them not to worry.

"They love me darling," he'd say. "Why would they want to hurt me?" Of course, he'd learned the hard way.

The atmosphere on the tour was wild—and getting wilder. At the Liverpool Empire, fans had rushed the stage and forced the management to bring down the safety curtain. The next night in Leeds, the same thing happened again, but this time Freddie managed to talk the fans back down into the auditorium.

By far the most raucous crowd of the tour, however, was the one that packed the Glasgow Apollo. I don't know if they were drunk or just excited, but they were so worked up they smashed the first ten rows of seats up. They were making a hell of a noise and were in a really agitated state.

Freddie hadn't really sussed what was going on, so early on in the gig he headed for the front of the stage. Suddenly, a big bloke in the audience grabbed hold of Freddie's microphone and lead and hauled him into the audience. Freddie had been a boxer at school and was tougher than he looked. But he wasn't a match for this ogre of a bloke. Poor old Freddie was suddenly lost in a sea of sweaty fans, some of whom were soon trying to divest him of his jewellery—and more. The bouncers had to go wading into the crowd to rescue him.

It really shook him up. Needless to say, he didn't make the same mistake twice. From then on, he stayed well away from the edge of the stage.

The tour came to an end at the famous Rainbow Theatre in North London. We'd decided to shoot a film of the two gigs there and spent the day before the gig making sure everything was just right.

Freddie, as usual, was being difficult. But on this particular day he was even more pedantic than usual.

Brian, who was still struggling with the after effects of his illness, took exception and told him as much.

"Oh stop being such a tart Freddie," he said loudly, making sure that everyone could hear.

Freddie was outraged. He just tossed back his head, waved his arms, and stormed off in a strop. The others didn't chase him—and nor did I. I had too much work to do with the director Bruce Gowers, and the crew Trilion had assembled to shoot the film together with the Trident team and Roy Baker to record the live album. We'd already begun filming some incidental footage of the band arriving in their limo and getting ready backstage. We wanted to be sure the gig itself was done justice.

For a while Freddie was nowhere to be seen. We all assumed he'd flounced off somewhere nearby and was lying low, brooding. It was a big theatre, so there were plenty of nooks and crannies to hide away. When it was time for the sound check Brian May got up on the stage and turned the mike on and took the volume right up, as high as it would go.

"Freddiepoos, where are you?" he shouted.

Everyone was pissing themselves with laughter, waiting to see what Freddie would do. He appeared almost immediately with a face like thunder. He was livid, seething. He flounced on stage, gave Brian a vicious look—and then just got on with it. That's what they always did. In that respect they were the ultimate pros.

Freddie's professionalism was actually called upon again that night. The theatre was packed to capacity, with 3,500 people in there.

The band was determined to try all sorts of things. Roger had decided that he was going to soak his drum kit in beer so that it sprayed everywhere when he hit them. He reckoned it made them sound better too, although no one was quite sure of that.

The other thing they had going on that night involved a huge amount of smoke and dry ice, which would be released at certain moments in the act. Unfortunately, at some point during the day, someone from the Rainbow's maintenance staff had left a backstage door open in the upper level of the theatre.

So when all the smoke grenades and guns went off, everything was being sucked across the stage up to the door. The result was chaos—the stage was suddenly engulfed in smoke. Freddie was on stage playing the piano at the time. He couldn't see the keys, let alone the rest of the band. It was like being in a fog. But somehow he got through it.

Queen played the Rainbow for two nights, and by the end Bruce Gowers and I were certain we had a pretty good film. There were some great elements to it—from the opening of the show in which a solitary spotlight picked out the figure of Freddie standing in the middle of the stage singing "Now I'm Here", to the rousing finale of "Liar", "Stone Cold Crazy", and "Lap of the Gods".

In the studio afterwards we spent two nights editing it into a live show. We decided to try an experiment and use the same system that had been used some years earlier on Frank Zapper's "200 Motels.

We had discussions with Rank films to act as distributor, who were keen to show it as the supporting feature for a new Burt Reynolds film. It was a first for the rock 'n' roll industry. Not even The Beatles or The Rolling Stones had had a film of a live concert shown nationwide at the cinema.

To mark both this success and the end of the tour, we threw a big party at the Holiday Inn at Swiss Cottage. Everyone let their hair down, and Mel Bush, who had promoted the tour, presented the boys with a brass plaque to mark the fact that they'd sold out every gig on the tour.

It should have been a time for the band to really sit back and enjoy their success. But there was something holding them back still.

They had always been a nervous band. And with more touring to come overseas, it was clear they were already fretting about that.

The problems Brian's illness had caused last time were at the root of their insecurity. Their UK tour had been a relatively small affair. In the coming weeks they were due to head off into Europe, where they were set to play in Scandinavia, Belgium, and Germany, supported by an up-and-coming American band called Lynyrd Skynyrd.

As it turned out, the band were right to be twitchy. It turned out to be another touring disaster, but for very different reasons this time.

Whilst travelling in Sweden, one of the tour trucks with all of the equipment on board missed a sign telling the driver to detour in order to avoid a low bridge.

It ploughed into a railway bridge, which opened up the truck like a tin can, spilling most of the PA system onto the road and wrecking the truck.

I got a phone call about it in the middle of the night.

I had no idea what to do. Fortunately Barry's wife was Swedish, so I phoned him. He made a few calls and, to my surprise and relief, it turned out that one of his Swedish relatives had a trucking company. They took a fleet of vans to where the wrecked truck was parked and shifted the equipment. We didn't get off scot-free. We had to cancel one gig after missing a ferry crossing. But it could have been a lot worse. The joys of touring! That particular excursion cost us dearly.

The boys returned from Europe knowing that early in the New Year they'd be heading back to the States for a big tour in which they'd be the headlining act. It had already been re-arranged once because of Brian's illness. The other three were all worried that Brian wouldn't be well enough to make it through the arduous tour, especially with all the travelling. As it turned out, they had good cause for concern— except their anxieties were being concentrated on the wrong person.

~

The boys headed out to the States in January of 1975. They were due to play forty-eight gigs there before taking a break in Hawaii and then heading off to Japan, where we'd set up some more concerts.

The biggest problem on their last overseas tour around Europe had been logistical. Their equipment truck had been involved in an accident, so they'd had to cancel some of the gigs.

Things went a lot more smoothly in America, on the logistics front at least. The tour kicked off in Columbus, Ohio, where Kansas and Mahogany Rush supported the boys. From there they were due to move on to Cincinnati, Dayton, Cleveland, Toledo, and Detroit. The crowds were huge. "Killer Queen" had been a top five single in the States and excitement at the gigs was high. Tickets had sold so well that extra dates had been added. They were soon playing two shows in a day, and to sell-out crowds. With Jack Nelson and Dave Thomas running the tour for us, it all seemed to be going like clockwork. There were no problems with the rigs or the pyrotechnics. And the sound and production quality at all the venues was as good as anyone could have wished for. The telexes and phone calls that were coming back to London were all full of good news. Of course, it couldn't last.

It wasn't long before the extra workload was taking its toll on the band. But it wasn't Brian who was struggling this time.

By the time the band was on the second leg of the tour, which took in cities like Boston, New York, and Philadelphia, Freddie was having trouble with his voice.

A similar situation had developed when they'd toured Europe a couple of months earlier. Freddie had developed a really bad cough, which had affected his vocal performance slightly. Dave Thomas and the rest of the tour management hadn't thought too much about it. He'd rested over Christmas and by the New Year seemed to be back to his old vocal self.

But now it had flared up again. On stage he was struggling to hit the really high notes and had to sing part of the show in a lower register. He was a pro, and got away with it. But he was also a perfectionist and hated the fact he wasn't singing at a hundred percent. Freddie being Freddie, he blamed everything for the problem, in particular the air conditioning in his rooms. Jack and Dave did everything they could to help him, but the problem was soon deteriorating.

After the second of the two gigs they were to play in Philadelphia, Freddie was so hoarse he could barely speak. Normally Freddie was the first to arrive and the last to leave the after-show partying. He was a party animal, much more than any of the rest of the band. But he knew he had a problem and had begun going to bed much, much earlier and sleeping a good ten hours. After the Philly gig, he rested for the night again but was no better when he woke up. In fact he was worse: he couldn't speak at all now.

Jack Nelson and Dave Thomas were in charge of the big decisions, and opted to get some medical advice. So while the rest of the band headed off to Washington for the next gig that night, Freddie went off with Jack and Dave to see a throat specialist at the University City Hospital. Back in London, we were kept fully up to speed with what was going on and were soon getting regular calls and messages.

The prognosis shocked us all. The consultant told Freddie that he thought he might have two nodes in his throat. This was the most likely reason why he'd strained his voice, he said. When Freddie asked him what he should do, the specialist said he shouldn't sing and should speak as little as possible for the next three months!

You can imagine his reaction. For a while he was hysterical, but when he calmed down his main emotion was depression. How could this have happened? Freddie was a complex character. As well as being a drama queen, he was also a real team player. He felt a deep responsibility to the rest of the band. As they headed out of the hospital, all he could keep saying was that he felt like he'd let the rest of the boys down. "The band will kill me," he said to Jack and Dave.

Rather than ringing the rest of the band with the news, Freddie, Jack, and Dave decided to wait to tell them face to face. They were due to appear that night in Washington at the John F. Kennedy Center. Freddie was determined that the show would go on. He couldn't face the idea of letting down a sell-out audience so late in the day. He'd sing that night then, and make a decision about his throat afterwards.

The only problem was that getting to Washington was now a problem. By the time they got to Philadelphia station it was late in the day. A few miles outside Baltimore the train suddenly came to a grinding halt. They were told they'd have to get off because there had been a major derailment.

Of course, this sent Freddie into a major flap. Jack and Dave tried to sort it out. But by the time they'd walked with all their gear to the nearest railway station every taxi and rental car had been booked. To make matters worse, a heavy fog made it so they couldn't schedule a flight or hire a private plane to Washington.

At five o'clock that afternoon—with just three hours to go before the concert—it looked like they were doomed. Freddie's mood had become almost inconsolable. But then, out of nowhere, there was an announcement that there was a single train making its way to Washington. They tried to book seats but were told there was no room.

Jack took an executive decision and booked two sleeping compartments at enormous cost. The three of them spent the slow journey to Washington lying in their cabins, fretting about whether they'd make it in time.

It was a close-run thing. They had obviously missed the afternoon sound check, but they reached the hotel where the rest of the band were waiting at 7.15 p.m.—three quarters of an hour before the gig.

Freddie, Jack, and Dave broke the news to the rest of the guys.

They were shocked, but determined like Freddie that that night's show should go on.

Apparently it was one of the best gigs they ever played. They were so fired up they nearly blew the roof off the place—and Freddie's vocals were perfect, even on the highest notes.

Despite this, however, Jack made the decision to pull the plug on five concerts. We contacted the promoters in Pittsburgh, Buffalo, London, Kutzron, Toronto, and Davenport to break the bad news. They weren't pleased—obviously.

The truth, however, was that it was our only option. It would give them a little more breathing space to tackle the Freddie situation and I told Jack to do whatever was required to look after him.

As it turned out, his problem wasn't quite as bad as it had been first feared. In Washington, he went to see another throat specialist. This one didn't think it was nodes that were causing the problem. He just thought it was a swelling that would calm down if he rested his voice.

We weren't sure which way to turn after that, so we decided to get a third opinion, this time from a specialist in New York who'd advised people like Barbra Streisand and Tom Jones. He too said it was a swelling rather than nodes.

Encouraged by this, the boys took some time off and then resumed the tour in La Crosse. They then headed for the west coast and the final leg of the tour. That proved to be an eventful few weeks—again for different reasons.

In Seattle, Freddie walked into his room one night to discover a lady there. It turned out she wasn't a fan or a groupie, but a burglar. She was rifling through his clothes and luggage and had stuffed her pockets with part of Freddie's extensive jewellery collection.

Freddie knew how to look after himself and wasn't intimidated. When she bolted for the door he chased her out of the room, down the corridor, and all the way into the lobby, screaming "stop thief" all the way. Luckily the security guys in the lobby heard his screaming and apprehended the woman.

There were some lighter moments, however. On stage in Santa Monica, John split his trousers midway through the set. Freddie thought this was hilarious and pointed it out to the entire audience. John was mortified and spent the first part of the set blushing like crazy.

The boys made it through most of the final leg, but had to cancel the last gig in Portland, Oregon, again because of Freddie's voice. As the tour drew to a close, they had played 33 out of forty-eight concerts. A third of the gigs had to be cancelled.

It was terrible news for us financially.. We'd hired an enormous amount of equipment out there at huge cost. That would still have to be paid for, regardless. We had also lost out on the ticket sales, of course. Pretty soon we began to see that—far from making the band and us a big profit—the tour was going to barely break even.

It also meant that we had a really big decision to make. Queen had been booked to go on to tour Japan, where we'd done a deal with the giant Watanabe Company and Warners. Queen were selling enormous volumes of records over there. Sheer Heart Attack and "Killer Queen" were both top of their respective charts. The Japanese were deadly keen to see them perform live. We'd been promised they'd be given a welcome like they'd never seen before.

It all sounded great, but we faced a real risk with Freddie's voice in such a delicate condition. Back at Trident, we hummed and hawed about it for hours on end. Should we pull the plug and cut our losses, or should we press on? The boys, needless to say, wanted to carry on.

They felt frustrated at not having really cracked America in the way they'd hoped. And they'd been hearing amazing things from Japan via their fan club. They really wanted to play there.

It was Jack who had the idea of sending them off to Hawaii for an extended break while all their gear and equipment was being shipped out to Japan. Rest had worked before with Brian, and the doctors were telling us that was what Freddie needed too. Jack's plan was that the boys would go direct from Hawaii to Tokyo, rather than coming back to the UK. It turned out to be one of the most significant decisions that we were ever to make—for all sorts of reasons.

The reception they received in Tokyo was beyond anything any of us had anticipated. They couldn't believe it. When they emerged through customs, they found 3,000 fans waiting for them, all dressed in Queen t-shirts, waving Queen banners and albums and chanting the band's name. Freddie's face had apparently been a picture.

Their first gig was at the giant Budokan hall in Tokyo. It was utter madness. The ten thousand tickets had apparently sold out in hours. The fans were going nuts.

The organisers had hired a group of giant Sumo wrestlers to control the growing crowds, but even they were soon struggling.

No sooner had Freddie and the boys stepped onto the stage than a wave of young fans, mostly girls, started surging around, moving from side to side and crashing into the front of the stage.

Freddie realised immediately that it was dangerous and stopped the gig. Through an interpreter he asked them all to calm down before someone got seriously hurt. Being good, courteous Japanese girls, they did—thankfully. The rest of the gig, which was being filmed live for a major Japanese television company, passed off without any more trouble.

It was the same for the next eleven days as they played a gig every day around the country. Wherever they went there were hordes of hysterical fans. They had to be smuggled in and out of the auditoria in armed vehicles. It was bonkers, like Beatlemania.

As a thank you to the fans, the boys came on stage for the last concert dressed in kimonos —which went down a storm.

By the time they were ready to come back from Japan, in April 1975, we all knew they'd reached a tipping point. It was a huge moment for the band, really the beginning of their global success. It was the first time that they'd been recognised as a major rock 'n' roll act. There was even a special awards ceremony organised by the magazine Music Life to present them with all sorts of gold discs and stuff to recognise their phenomenal sales in Japan.

Freddie in particular was overwhelmed by the reception and the genuine love he felt directed at him. In Japan he'd finally found the acclaim and adulation he'd craved all his life. He felt like a God. Unfortunately for me and for Trident, Freddie would soon start behaving like one too . . .

1972 (p.204-205) **LEFT PAGE:** *Full page:* Brian May and Roger Taylor listening to playback in Trident's remix room .
RIGHT PAGE: *Top:* Roger Taylow, Freddie Mercury and Brian May singing into a classic Neumann Trident Microphone. Bottom right: 8 track cassette of Queen's Sheer Heart Attack.

1974 (p.206-207) **LEFT PAGE:** Top & middle far left: Freddie Mercury performs at the Rainbow Theatre North London. *Middle left:* The Rainbow smoke machine adding to the Stage "Atmosphere". *Middle right:* Queen performing. *Far right:* Queen's first Album Sleeve. *Bottom:* The Rainbow light show.
RIGHT PAGE: *(clockwise)* Roger Taylor, Brain May, Freddie Mercury, John Deacon performing. The video of this famous Rainbow gig was recorded by Trilion and later released on VHS.

1974 (p.208-209) **LEFT PAGE:** (clockwise) *Top left:* Mott the Hoople original tour poster. *Top right:* Official signed press photograph on Queen's return from Japan. *Bottom:* Queen celebrating with Mott the Hoople and the infamous cake scene. *Middle left:* Freddie Mercury and Brian May perfoming.
RIGHT PAGE: (clockwise) *Top:* Freddie Mercury performing . *Middle row:* Sales awards presented to Trident for 'Queen'. *Queen II', 'Sheer Heart Attack' and 'A Night at the Opera'. Middle bottom right:* Queen Sheer Heart Attack cover, Bottom right: Backstage party invite celebrating the end of the Magic Tour which became the last ever Queen show. *Bottom left:* Queen at Trident's Offices.

1974

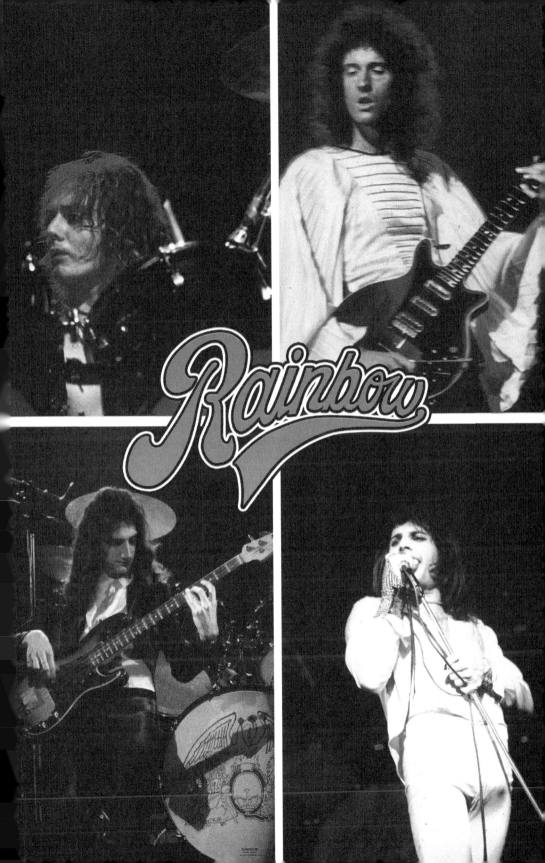

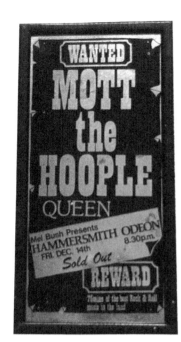

Queen

1974

QUEEN SHEER HEART ATTACK

THIS INVITATION ADMITS YOU
TO THE BACKSTAGE ARTISTS COMPOUND
AFTER THE SHOW TO CELEBRATE
THE END OF THE

QUEEN
MagicTour
OF EUROPE

DRESS - CASUAL
FUN FACTOR - HIGH!

KNEBWORTH PARK   ADMIT ONE   9th AUGUST 10.45 pm

The Contracts

Queen Original Recording, Management & Assignments Contracts

PLFF No: 2'

A N   A G R E E M E N T   made this   first   day

of November   One thousand nine hundred and Seventy-two

                                                    17 St. Anne's
B E T W E E N   NEPTUNE PRODUCTIONS LIMITED   of ~~Max Harcourt~~

~~Street~~ Court, W.1. Greater London (hereinafter called "the

Company") of the one part and FREDERICK BULSARA   of ▓▓▓▓▓▓▓

▓▓▓▓▓▓▓▓▓▓▓▓▓▓▓▓▓▓▓▓▓▓ London ~~X.X.8.~~ W.14. JOHN RICHARD DEACON

of ▓▓▓▓▓▓▓▓▓▓▓▓▓▓▓▓▓▓▓London S.W.7. BRIAN HAROLD MAY

of ▓▓▓▓▓▓▓▓▓▓▓▓▓▓▓▓▓London S.W.~~X~~7. and ROGER MEDDOWS

TAYLOR of ▓▓▓▓▓▓▓▓▓▓▓▓▓▓▓▓▓▓▓▓▓▓▓▓▓▓ (hereinafter

collectively called "the Artist") of the other part

20. THE parties acknowledge that the Company has
provided or purchased for the Artist goods and
equipment having an agreed value of SIX THOUSAND POUNDS
                                   6000
(~~£3000~~) which sum shall be treated as a non-returnable
advance against royalties hereafter accruing due to
the Artist and which advance the Company shall be
entitled to recoup our of royalties accruing to the
Artist hereunder

AS WITNESS the hands of the parties hereto
the day and year first above mentioned_____

SIGNED ON BEHALF OF NEPTUNE)
PRODUCTIONS LIMITED

SIGNED BY THE ABOVE-NAMED)
ARTIST

THIS AGREEMENT is made the first PLFF No: 3
day of November One thousand nine hundred and Seventy-two
BETWEEN TRIDENT AUDIO PRODUCTIONS LTD.,
~~JOHN HARDING NELSON~~ of ~~14 Wardour Street~~ 17 St. Anne's Court,
W.1. Greater London (hereinafter called "the Manager") of
the one part and FREDERICK BULSARA of
~~Kensington~~ London W.14. JOHN RICHARD DEACON of
London S.W.7. BRIAN HAROLD MAY of
London S.W.7. and ROGER MEDDOWS TAYLOR of
~~London S.W.18.~~ (collectively called
"QUEEN" and hereinafter referred to as "the Artist" of
the other part

2. THE Manager's duties hereunder shall be whenever called upon so to do to guide and advise the Artist with respect to his career and to act for him as Manager and Personal Representative in all matters concerning the Artist's interests in the entertainment industry. Without prejudice to the generality of the foregoing the Manager shall also attend to such advertising and publicity of the Artist as the Manager may consider necessary but he shall not spend thereon more than TEN POUNDS (£10) in any one calendar month without the Artist's authority

10. THE Manager agrees to advance to the Artist the sum of ONE HUNDRED POUNDS (£100) per week for a period of twelve months all of which monies shall be recoupable by the Manager out of all or any receipts of the Artist

SIGNED by the Manager in the presence of :-

London, Y.W.C.

P.P. TRIDENT AUDIO PRODUCTIONS LIMITED

SIGNED by the Artist in the presence of :-

FREDERICK BULSARA

JOHN RICHARD DEACON

BRIAN HAROLD MAY

ROGER MEDDOWS TAYLOR

THIS ASSIGNMENT is made the 28th day of March One thousand nine hundred and seventy seven BETWEEN NEPTUNE PRODUCTIONS LIMITED of 36/44 Brewer Street London W1R 3FW (hereinafter called "Neptune") of the first part TRIDENT AUDIO PRODUCTIONS LIMITED of 36/44 Brewer Street London W1R 3FW (hereinafter called "Trident") of the second part CENTREDISC LIMITED of 36/44 Brewer Street London W1R 3FW (hereinafter called "Centredisc") of the third part NORMAN SHEFFIELD of 36/44 Brewer Street London W1R 3FW in his capacity as a Director of Neptune Trident and Centredisc (hereinafter called "Mr. Sheffield") of the fourth part and FREDERICK MERCURY JOHN RICHARD DEACON BRIAN HAROLD MAY ROGER MEDDOWS TAYLOR all care of Moore Sloane & Co. 201 Holland Park Avenue London W11 4UN (hereinafter together called "Queen") of the fifth part

WHEREAS

(b)   to release Queen from any further obligation regarding Queen's agreement referred to in Recital (3)(b) with respect to the Trident logo and wording (such logo and wording hereinafter together referred to as "the Trident Logo") on the terms and conditions hereinafter contained

(6)   The parties hereto acknowledge that:-

(i)   the Management Debt (consisting of expenses paid on behalf of and advances paid to Queen by Trident) has been recouped by Trident and totals the sum of £303,392.71 and therefore

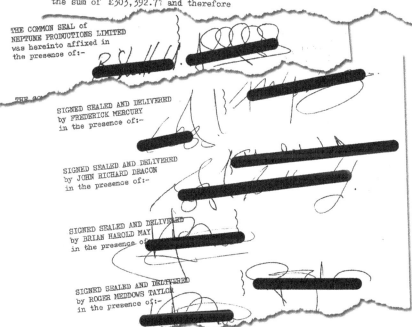

THE COMMON SEAL of
NEPTUNE PRODUCTIONS LIMITED
was hereinto affixed in
the presence of:-

THE CO

SIGNED SEALED AND DELIVERED
by FREDERICK MERCURY
in the presence of:-

SIGNED SEALED AND DELIVERED
by JOHN RICHARD DEACON
in the presence of:-

SIGNED SEALED AND DELIVERED
by BRIAN HAROLD MAY
in the presence of:-

SIGNED SEALED AND DELIVERED
by ROGER MEDDOWS TAYLOR
in the presence of:-

Twelve

I Want It All, And I Want It Now

"We'll go to Harrods and buy it cash so everyone can see it."

I was sitting in the Trident offices one afternoon in May of 1975 when Freddie Mercury sailed in. As usual these days, it was quite an entrance. It was a bit like an ancient Roman emperor returning, triumphant from a distant war, which in a way he was.

He was wearing a fur coat and was weighed down with presents for the girls in the office. As they gathered around him he began producing stuff out of a giant case. There were expensive-looking silk kimonos, fans, lacquered boxes, and bits of jewellery. Freddie being Freddie, it was all high-class stuff. There was no tat from the airport or flea markets. He'd probably bought it all at Japan's best antiques markets. He had even splashed out on an old, Samurai sword for himself, he announced.

"And whose money paid for that little lot?" I thought to myself.

There wasn't anything for me, of course. Why would there be? I was only the mug who'd paid for a large chunk of the trip.

With all the bills in, we knew that the Japanese tour had cost us in the region of £60,000 (c.£520,000). While Warners and Wattanabe had picked up their chunk of the promotion and staging costs, we'd met all the tour costs—including Freddie's shopping expeditions.

Still, I told myself that it was worth it, certainly in terms of publicity and promotion. And it would definitely pay off in Japanese record sales further down the line. It was all adding to the positive future we and Queen had in front of us. Or so I thought . . .

The boys had been back a while now and had been busy for much of the month, working on new material and collecting awards. Their records were still selling phenomenally well and they were beginning to get the recognition they craved. Early in May, they had won top band at that year's Disc Magazine awards. It was one of four awards. They also won for best live group, British group, international group, and best single for "Killer Queen". Days later Freddie had won another award, a rather prestigious one known as the Ivor Novello award which was presented by the Songwriters Guild of Great Britain for his work on "Killer Queen". He was totally delighted.

Freddie had already been talking to the press, so I knew a bit about his frame of mind.

He'd been talking effusively about how well it had gone in Japan, where, as he kept saying, they'd been treated "like demi-Gods".

Freddie told a story about how they had all been given personal bodyguards by the promoters, Wattanabe. Freddie had been amused by the fact that his had been a judo and karate expert who had been no more than four feet two inches tall.

The hardest thing, he said, was coming back down to earth and going back to his little flat in Kensington where he was once again "making his own cups of tea". He was also still suffering from the throat troubles he'd picked up in America, probably exacerbated by the long flight back from Tokyo. I knew there was nothing more dangerous than a fragile Freddie with time on his hands. So when, after distributing his gifts all around the office, he stuck his head in and said, in a rather ominous tone that he and his advisors "really needed" to have a meeting with me, I had an inkling about what was about to come my way.

The more successful they'd become, the more agitated Queen had grown about the money situation with Trident. They were always an insecure band. I think they needed something to worry about. In America it had been Freddie's health. Now, back in London, it was money and the way things were going with their career. Despite the adulation they'd felt in Japan, they were convinced there were problems.

Things had come to a head with Jack Nelson in recent months. Since the American tour, relations between him and the band had deteriorated badly. They'd told me they didn't want to work with him, and he'd agreed to quit as their manager. He'd already headed back to the States. I'd been upset at their attitude towards him. No one had worked harder to get them their first breaks. But I knew there was nothing I could do to retrieve the situation. Freddie and Jack, in particular, were no longer on speaking terms.

I'd already had a preliminary talk with the band about finding new management. They'd agreed to have a think about who they might like to look after them.

I'd also said I'd consider some candidates. In the short term, Dave Thomas would look after their day-to-day needs, I would look after the "big picture", dealing with EMI, Elektra in the US, and everyone else around the world.

The breakdown in the relationship had been partly to do with personalities, of course. But more than that, I knew it had been about money. Or more accurately, the boys' perceived lack of it. There was nothing particularly new in this, of course. We'd had showdowns about money before, lots of them.

One of the most heated had come earlier that year, just before they'd gone off to the States, when John Deacon got married. He'd arranged to marry his long-time girlfriend, Veronica Tetzlaff, at the Carmelite Church on Kensington High Street. In the run up to it he'd announced that he wanted me to spring £10,000 (c.£100,000) so that he could buy a house for the pair of them and the child they were expecting. I must admit I didn't react too well. I gave him short shrift.

"You've got your girlfriend pregnant and you want to get married. Is it my fault?" I said. "I know I'm your mother and your father, but I'm not your bank." As you can imagine, that went down like a lead balloon.

Soon after that, Roger had asked for money to buy a car. My reaction had been similarly forthright. "Buy one with your own money," I told him.

Then, not long after that, Freddie had demanded a grand piano. Of course, that was the fiercest argument of all. Freddie didn't react well to being told no. So when I'd turned him down, he'd banged his fist on my desk.

"I have to get a grand piano," he'd said.

I'd tried to reason with him.

"For a start Freddie, how you are going to get a bloody grand piano in a flat in Kensington. Are you going to take the windows out?" I said.

He just glared at me.

"I know, we'll make a publicity stunt out of it," he came back. "We'll go to Harrods and buy it cash so everyone can see it."

I just laughed.

"I'm not taking cash to Harrods. Apart from anything else the taxman would have your guts for garters," I said. "If you really want to do a stunt out of it, we'll take monopoly money."

I wasn't being mean. I was simply trying to be businesslike. The way the music publishing industry worked, it took a good year or two for money to start flowing through the royalty system. We knew there was a huge amount of money due to come flooding our way from Queen's success. Some of it was already coming in, but the vast majority of it hadn't arrived yet, and wouldn't for a few months yet, probably until October.

I'd explained this to the boys until I was blue in the face. But, as we gathered in the office, a few days later, I had to do it all over again. By now they'd all employed accountants and a lawyer to handle their affairs. They were claiming that they were due money—large sums of money. Freddie had even alluded to this in his press interviews back here in the UK. He'd talked about how he was keen to find out how much money he'd made as a result of Queen's success.

As we sat there around a boardroom table, I explained that the first royalty cheques had begun to come in from EMI. But at that point they were relatively small, certainly compared to what we expected to get later in the year. And in any case they had been soaked up by the costs of running the growing Queen empire.

In the run up to the last tours of the UK, Europe, the US, and Japan, for instance, we'd decided that we'd invest £30,000 (c.£300,000) in a lighting rig like no one had seen before in their life. The US tour itself had also cost £34,000, and—because of Freddie's illness—had failed to make a profit or even break even, although in this case it would come back in record sales as and when the royalties arrived.

I could see the look on their faces. It was as if they were shocked to hear this. I wasn't having it. "We had a meeting previously and everyone had agreed—that's where the money would go I said. "We did it and it worked- I have totally put my neck on the line for you guys"

But, once again, it went in one ear and out the other. As the conversation went around the room, they all moaned about not having any cash despite the fact they were at the top of the charts. At this point I lost my temper slightly, something that—perhaps—I regret looking back on it.

"Don't whinge about not having any money, you've had loads of money and you've spent it look at all the equipment that you wanted and the stuff you brought back from Japan."

"But we're stars. I've just won an Ivor Novello award. We're selling millions of records," Freddie said. "And I'm still living in the same bloody flat I've been living in for the past three years."

Again, I had to burst their bubble and bring them back to earth. That was my job.

"No, we think we've sold millions of records," I said. "But we don't know yet."

Once again I explained the cold, unglamorous financial reality to them. We'd made the investment. The four and half years of hard work had paid off. We were now ready to make some money. All they had to do was be a little patient, - the next royalties would arrive in October just a few months away. I was certain they would soon be very rich young men.

But when it came to money, it wasn't that they didn't get it. They didn't want to get it.

It was a track we'd been round before, ad nauseam. But as the meeting broke up this time, however, I got the distinct feeling that there was something different about their mood now. I sensed something in the wind. It wasn't long before I got confirmation of what it was . . .

One day, not long after that meeting, I looked up to see a familiar face walking into my office. It was Don Arden, as usual with an Al Capone-sized cigar in his mouth, He really was getting to look more and more like a parody of the Godfather.

"Hello Don," I said. "Always a pleasure to see you. What can I do you for?"

My sarcasm was wasted on him. He plonked himself down in a chair, pulled out a piece of paper and came straight out with it.

"It's Queen," he said. "They've asked me to take them over. They're finished with you lot. You're out of the picture."

He then slapped this document on the table. I could see it was some kind of contractual thing. It looked like it had been signed by the band.

If it had come from a more respected figure in the music business, I'd have been worried. But Don Arden was another matter. I didn't believe it for a minute. And even if it was true, he was the last person on earth I'd let manage Queen.

"Don," I said, handing the document back to him, "you can take that, get out of here, and down the corridor you'll find a toilet. Take it in there and you can wipe your backside on it."

He growled at me and refused to move.

"Look, it's here in black and white. I sat down and had a good talk with the boys in America when they were out there on tour. They're not happy with what you're doing for them and they want someone to do the job properly. Freddie's really keen. There's nothing you can do about it," he said.

"Yes, there is," I said. "I'll just put the band on suspension and that will be the end of it. Everyone will be up shit creek. That's the last thing I want to do. We'll negotiate with them over a new management deal—but in our own time. And not with you."

Don wasn't prepared to back down. He rambled on about how he had got control of the band and was going to do this and that and the other.

"Don. No you're not," I said. "So just piss off and go and find someone else's band to play with."

It was, of course, all bravado on my part. Inside, I was shaken. Badly shaken. What was the band up to?

What the hell was going on? I got hold of Dave Thomas and tried to find out what he knew.

Dave confirmed that somehow Don Arden had spent some time with Queen while they were in the States.

"How the hell did that happen?" I said. "Where the hell was Jack?"

He didn't know, which suggested to me that Jack really had taken his eye off the ball somewhere along the line. It was probably for the best that he'd left the picture.

I could just picture the scene that had played out. I could see the oily figure of Don Arden sitting the boys down over a drink in some hotel bar and filling their head with all kinds of rubbish. I could hear him telling them how crap we were and how wonderful he was and what amazing things he was going to do for them. "You boys should be living in mansions and driving around in Rolls Royce's by now." Worst of all, I could imagine Freddie and the boys nodding along. I could hear them whinging about us.

For the record, we paid for our homes, cars and expenses out of our own salaries, which were drawn from the various companies that we owned and not from Queen. They couldn't contribute anything at that time, as the company that related to them, Trident Audio Productions, was still hugely overdrawn.

Getting Queen to sign that piece of paper must have been as easy as shooting fish in a barrel.

What I didn't understand was how Don Arden had got wind of the problems we were having with Queen. I knew America was a place where people were always hustling and chancing their arm. But why had he muscled in over there? Dave mentioned something about Don's daughter Sharon liking Freddie and wanting him to sign them up for her. That sounded a bit unlikely to me, for all sorts of reasons!

That wasn't the really big issue now, however. The thing that troubled me was that the cat was out of the bag. And I knew that if Don Arden knew there was trouble brewing with Queen then everyone would know. And I knew everyone would want to get their hands on them. I had to act. And fast.

~

The news hit me hard. For days afterwards, I kept analysing the situation going over every twist and turn in the past few months. If I was honest, it wasn't entirely out of the blue. Quite the opposite, in fact. For a start, it was precisely what I'd always predicted was going to happen if they had their publishing, recording, and management all tied in together.

Somewhere along the line, there was going to be a situation where the band's management was going to want one thing and the band's publishers or record company would want another. That couldn't happen in our case because they were, to all intents and purposes, the same people. It was a conflict of interests—it was always going to be when the band became successful, just as I had prophesied in 1972.

Regardless of that, I felt like I was personally responsible for the breakdown in relations with Queen. Trident had become such a big operation—we were now eleven companies—that my energies had become divided. The buck stopped with me, I had too many other things on my mind to oversee it all. The band could have done with more of my time—full time. I regretted it now because I could already see that there was a danger we weren't going to capitalise on all the hard work we had done. We'd done everything right—but I just had this nagging feeling that we could have done it better.

The situation left me with a huge problem. How were we going to move forward without endangering the huge investment we'd made in the band? We still had their recording and publishing contracts. We had to protect them.

The nuclear option was to put the band on suspension while we sorted things out. That was a standard process in the industry. It was like arbitration—recording, touring, everything stops. During suspension everything is in limbo until it's sorted out. I knew that would be a disaster, particularly for a sensitive band like Queen.

The band were so temperamental in those days, they were so on the edge that I didn't want to go down that route. It would have destroyed them. Freddie was so temperamental he'd have gone off in a huff. Brian would have gone back to study.

Roger would have remained a rock 'n' roll star. John would have gone back to electronics. But the band would have collapsed.

So I decided not to do it. Instead, I decided on a couple of things. First off, I needed to get to the bottom of what Queen were feeling and talk to them about their new management. As it turned out, one of the first things I found out was that they'd already dismissed the idea of working with Don Arden. I was pretty certain that Freddie had been the one who had instigated the idea of them joining Don. Over in the States it had probably seemed like a good idea. But back in London, Brian, John, and Roger had seen through the bullshit. They'd probably also asked around about Don and discovered his reputation. That was the good news. In a way the even better news was that they'd started thinking about a few other names as potential managers. It was a short list, but it included people like Peter Rudge, who looked after 10cc; Peter Grant, Led Zeppelin's manager; and John Reid, Elton John's guiding spirit. It was a good list, one that I was happy about. John Reid, in particular, seemed like a perfect fit for Queen—and Freddie.

I felt sure that Trident would remain part of Queen's publishing and recording life and I felt confident that we'd be able to work with any of those three guys.

But the main thing I told them was to continue working. The boys were already at work on a fourth album. "Just keep working, keep working," I said. "Trident will continue to finance everything. We'll find a way through this."

And at that point I really believed we would. I really did.

With all the dramas surrounding Queen, it was hard sometimes to remember that I was still running a phenomenally successful group of companies with incredibly talented staff. Some of the best recording artists in the world were passing through our doors every day. Inevitably, some of them brought us highs—while others brought us lows.

We would always have our share of "challenging" artists.

Speaking of which, Rod Stewart recorded with us around this time—briefly.

He'd only been there a few days when I got a phone call in the office to go down to the studio.

"We think you'd better see this Norman," one of the engineering team said.

Rod was always a lively character, but he was clearly going through some sort of problem at that time. He had decided to go around the studio drawing phallic symbols in black felt pen. These bloody things were all over the place—including the staircase and our extremely expensive, cloth wall finishes.

"Shit. This is going to cost a few bob to clean up and fix," I said, before telling Rod that he was only renting the place to make a record.

"If you want to draw graffiti you can go and work somewhere else," I said in no uncertain language.

I called up Rod's manager, my old colleague Billy Gaff, and said he had a large bill coming. He was not too pleased.

Not long afterwards Rod moved the sessions to the Record Plant studios in the US. Years later I heard that it had happened all over again.

Another artist who didn't have enough respect for the premises was Graham Bond, the jazz organist whose band the Graham Bond Organisation had included such great names as Ginger Baker, Jack Bruce, Alexis Korner, and John McLaughlin.

Bond was a great artist and liked to work in the dark by candlelight. Each to his own, of course, but not when the candles set fire to the wall curtain, which happened during one of his sessions!

That required another call to the artist's management and another new rule in the studio—no candles.

Another demanding artist was Vangelis, the Greek composer and musician who had arrived on the scene in the late sixties and early seventies with his former band Aphrodite's Child, which also included Demis Rusos. He was, in many ways, the embodiment of the very artistic, very experimental way the music industry was going. He and his musicians were certainly the complete opposite of the sort of band I'd played in. Whereas with The Hunters we'd always prepared songs to perfection before we stepped into a studio, Vangelis would arrive in the studio to write and rehearse his music.

He would come in and sit behind his Hammond organ, twiddling away and trying out loads of effects. If he liked something, he'd play around with it for three or four hours. But then often he'd decide it wasn't so good after all. It was, of course, something that fitted with Trident's original philosophy. But having said that, it was an incredibly difficult thing for the producers and engineers to handle, because they had to make sure they captured everything he put down—even if it was quite obviously crap.

Vangelis used to drive poor old Malcolm Toft crazy. He could never work out whether the stuff he and his musicians were playing was serious or whether it was just tinkering. Whenever he made a judgment on that, Sod's law dictated that he was wrong.

That was the precise moment that Vangelis would look up at the booth and say, "Did you get that Malcolm?"

Malcolm was actually offered a job by Vangelis after he recorded one album with us. It was a decent wage too, £60 a week. But he knew he couldn't do it. He never regretted the decision.

For every "challenging" act, of course, there was another that was an absolute pleasure. Around the same time as Vangelis recorded with us, Genesis were back in the studio. They were going through a major upheaval at the time. Their lead singer, Peter Gabriel, had quit the band and they were in laying down their seventh album, A Trick of the Tail. They were also in the process of looking for a replacement singer. It was like the search for Scarlett O'Hara in

Gone With The Wind. In all they saw something like four hundred different vocalists.

We knew and liked the Genesis boys a lot. We'd known them since their early days. A lot of us had a feeling that their new singer was actually sitting right under their noses. The band's drummer Phil Collins had been a popular figure at Trident. He'd always been someone who would chip in and give advice. He loved the atmosphere at the studio. Phil could actually sing, and had been given some vocal duties on their latest albums. But the band—and he—had been determined to find someone else.

By late autumn 1975, the band looked like they were getting close to finding a new member. A guy called Mick Stickland had come in and impressed Phil, Mike Rutherford, Steve Hackett, and Tony Banks. They were all ready to give him the job when he came in and tried to sing to the backing tracks they'd already laid down for A Trick of the Tail.

It proved a disaster. The guy could sing, there was no doubt about that. But his voice just didn't suit the material. It was all in completely the wrong key for him. He simply couldn't do it.

I remember being in the studio around this time, and they were getting a bit desperate. The deadline for finishing A Trick of the Tail was approaching. One night Phil said he'd come in the next day and give it a go.

He went in and tried singing one of the hardest songs on the album, "Squonk". He recalled afterwards that he was quite nervous about it. But, of course, he nailed it first time. There was a soft, melodic quality to his voice that just suited their music perfectly.

It confirmed what everyone had suspected all along.

During the session he kept looking up to the recording booth, where the other members of the band were listening to his vocals mixed in with the backing track. Whenever he did, all he could see was the image of one or more of them giving him a giant thumbs up.

As one of them said later, "We'd all been trying to avoid the obvious for so long, but after that there was no way we could." As everyone knows, Phil Collins went on to do rather well after that. If only every band dealt with change as well as Genesis, I thought to myself at the time.

~

In June 1975, I received a set of management accounts relating to Queen. I could see that there was going to be a parting of the ways, in at least one way or another. I had them drawn up in anticipation of us trying to knock out a settlement with their new management— whoever that might be.

The detailed accounts, which were extracted from the ledgers we had been keeping since we first signed the band up, made for some interesting reading, that's for sure.

The amounts of money we'd invested into the band were huge. The total figure which was accepted by them at the end of the whole process was £178,000 (c.£1 million), but the figure I had was closer to £190,000. But there were also other, separate outlays relating to non-music things. Queen at the Rainbow, for instance, had cost us another £30,000 (c.£300,000) but it produced a super live show and live album.

The specific figures would have made fascinating reading for a music journalist—or indeed any other journalist.

Among the reasonable and deductible sums we'd listed were items like £602 (c.£5,000) for damage to a room they'd stayed in whilst touring Japan. £602? How the hell did they manage that?

Then there were tips. The total figure was £1,600 (c.£14,000) over a three-year period. What the hell had these waiters and bellboys been doing for them?

The clothes bill was another figure that jumped out. It totalled £1,500 (c.£13,000). That figure didn't surprise me really, considering the way that Freddie constantly pestered me for new outfits for him and the rest of the band.

My only concern was that we were still spending money, hand over fist, in particular on their new album. They had already started work on their fourth album, which was going to be called A Night at the Opera. Apparently they'd watched the Marx Brothers film of that name one night when laying down some early tracks and decided it was a great album title.

Predictably they were no longer using Trident. They were recording at various locations, but in particular the Rockfield studios down in Monmouth in Wales, and Sarm in the West End. Roy Thomas Baker was producing, and he'd brought other Trident engineers along with him. But the fact that they were no longer working in-house was making it an extremely expensive business as we had no control.

Recording on the album began around August and was scheduled to go on until October, with the album due out in November that year. Given their success with Sheer Heart Attack, we were all pretty confident it was going to be big. Very big.

It was around September that we next sat down with Freddie and the boys and their representatives to try to work our way through the situation. All sorts of ideas had been floated in the past four months. The boys had engaged a lawyer, a called Jim Beach, to help negotiate their way through the minefield that a change of management would create.

For a while, they had thought about letting me take over control of the management. I had, after all, been the person they'd originally asked to guide their career years ago. I put it to them and they thought about it for a while. I think Brian and John were keen. But Freddie—I think—thought the trust between us had somehow been broken and killed the idea stone dead. I hadn't realised the anger and animosity he felt towards me—yet.

I wasn't too concerned about that. To be honest, I had more than an enough on my plate with Trident, Trilion, and everything else. I just wanted their new manager to be someone I was happy to be in bed with, so to speak.

Brian was particularly insistent about what sort of person was going to take over the management of the band. I listened carefully to everything he said, and was reasonably happy they were heading in the right direction. I had a very strong feeling they were going to go with John Reid.

People said to me afterwards, "Why were you bothered?" It was simple, I told them. After all the time, effort, and money we'd put in Queen was a huge investment for us. We'd given up the management at that point, but we retained the publishing rights and recording rights. So whoever the person was who would eventually take over the management, it was essential that they should be right for the job. We didn't want to see them wreck the other aspects of the Queen business

It may have been the fact that he was talking to other managers and hearing an alternative view of the world, but as we tried to talk things through, Freddie once more got it into his head that he was due a huge amount of money. The fact that the band owed Trident close to £200,000 (c.£1.75 million) simply didn't seem to register with him. Again he came out with that line about him being owed "millions". He was a star. He should be living like one. All the same old crap.

Again, sitting down in an office at Trident, I explained the reality to him. Firstly, they'd been paid increasing wages as an advance of royalties all the way through up until now. Secondly, we'd invested heavily in them when they didn't have a pot to piss in. We'd advanced them equipment and salaries right at the beginning and had continued to pour money into them for the past four years. On top of that, they had received record advances and other large chunks of money. But they had also agreed to re-invest that money in the band and their development. All that hard work was about to pay dividends. We weren't quite at the point where the money was going to arrive. But we were closer than ever.

I can remember the conversation almost verbatim.

"The returns come in October, the money comes in December," I said. "We can smell good, but we can't see good. EMI smells good as well, but even they can't be sure. So wait."

It was then, however, that I realised where we were headed. The atmosphere in the room was strangely subdued. There was a distinctly chilly atmosphere, which hadn't always been the case. Things often got very heated—literally, when we were having an argument. Somewhere, deep at the back of my mind, a penny was beginning to drop. It was clear that Freddie, Brian, Roger, and John were not prepared to wait any longer.

In fact, as it turned out, they weren't prepared to wait another moment.

It was a phrase that he would make famous around the world in years to come, although no one would have known where it was born.

As I tried once again to explain to Freddie why it was he'd have to wait two final months for his big payday, he stamped his feet and raised his voice.

"No, I am not prepared to wait any longer. I want it all. I want it now," he said. That was when I knew my relationship with Queen was over. . .

Thirteen

Death On Two Legs

"You are not going to like this at all, I think you had better listen to this track from the album, he told me."

The autumn and winter of 1975 and early 1976 were a period of huge highs and lows for Trident, Queen, and me. As Charles Dickens might have said: it was the best of times and the worst of times.

By now Queen had finally decided to ask John Reid to manage their career. He'd agreed and had got stuck in straight away. That had been a welcome bit of news as far as I was concerned. He was the kind of guy with whom I could do business. But his arrival had been quickly followed by another piece of news that hit Trident like a bombshell.

As I'd suspected after the bad-tempered meetings in September, the band, via Jim Beach, had announced that they wanted a complete break from Trident. That meant they didn't want us to be involved in their publishing or recording either.

Again, we tried to explain the implications to them. Through John Reid, we told them that we thought it was madness to leave when they were in such debt to us. And we pointed out that, in leaving, they were creating even more debt. Because we had the rights to their next four albums, we'd be due things contractually that related to earnings they hadn't even made yet. It was going to be a minefield. But they were determined to cut all ties. And with a new, independent management representing them, I knew there was going to be no talking them out of it.

That made life even more complicated—and the arguments even more heated. At this point, however, I made a decision that we were going to try to be as decent and gentlemanly about this as possible. If we'd been a big, hard-nosed American record label we'd have come down on them like a ton of bricks. We could have insisted on everything that was in the contracts and sued them to high heaven if they didn't deliver it. But we didn't operate that way—nor were we ever going to. We wanted to sort this out as amicably—and fairly as possible. I instructed a good lawyer, a guy called Ted Oldman, to look into getting some kind of severance deal which also allowed us to retain a percentage of their earnings on the albums they had already done for us and were contracted to do in the future. That included A Night at the Opera, of course.

This would help ensure that we didn't in any way interfere with recording. According to everything I was hearing via Roy Thomas Baker and everyone else, it was going really well. Why should we?

Facing up to the prospect that we were losing Queen was hard for me—and everyone else at Trident. We'd put so much time, money, and effort into developing them. It felt like a real kick in the teeth. But there was no point in dwelling on it—well, not now at least. We had to pick our way through it. It wasn't ever going to be pleasant. But it didn't have to be nasty. Well, that's what I thought anyway.

Pretty soon, I was hearing that the band was making all sorts of derogatory comments about Trident—and me in particular. They were saying I was making outrageous demands, which was bollocks.

With Ted Oldman we'd started to lay out what we felt we were owed by Queen. It was a big number—obviously. For a start, they still had three albums to go under their recording contract with us. They hadn't done their quota of six albums, which was calculated in their recording contract as 24 tracks per year

So we came up with a figure for estimated royalties due on the next four albums, including A Night at the Opera. We knew they didn't have the cash to pay so we took what's called an "over ride" on it, and on top of that we gave them time to pay. How fair could we be?

We also said we were open to selling back the rights to their earlier albums when they had some money. In the end we agreed to hang on to them for a year, allowing them to buy them back in instalments.

I thought it was all going as well as it could. But again, I'd underestimated the depth of feeling within the band—and within Freddie Mercury in particular.

~

I'd deliberately stayed out of the way during the recording of A Night at the Opera. But towards the end, as it was finally edited, it came back to Trident to be finished off. So I couldn't resist sticking my head in and listening as it all came together.

Although relations were strained, they were still civil. And I was professional enough to know that what they'd recorded was going to be an enormous success. The album was extremely adventurous. A song called "Bohemian Rhapsody" stood out in particular—an epic, operatic piece which Freddie had written.

But then Dave Thomas arrived at my office one day.

"You are not going to like this at all, I think you had better listen to this track from the album," he told me.

We stuck it on. It was called "Death on Two Legs". The moment I heard it—and more importantly—read the lyrics, I knew what it was about.

The opening two lines summed up what was to come. "You suck my blood like a leech/you break the law and you breach." It went on to rage against a "misguided old mule" with "pigheaded rules" and "narrow minded cronies".

"Do you feel like suicide?" it went on. "I think that you should."

Brian had, apparently, been shocked when he'd heard this for the first time. He felt bad singing it because it felt "so vindictive" but sadly agreed to use it on the album regardless.

I felt no consideration had been given to me and all the Trident crew that had helped them so far.

There was no doubt in my mind that it was some kind of nasty hate mail from Freddie to me. We were, after all, in the midst of a long, protracted and increasingly bad-tempered negotiation.

But it really didn't merit that. I got Ted Oldman to send a legal letter to EMI.

He made it clear that Trident were responsible for and controlled the publishing of Queen material and we should have seen all of the lyrics from either the band or from our publishers, EMI Music, prior to the publishing.

But there was more to it than that. The band had committed a libel against me.

(I should state here that neither Freddie nor any other member of the band have made any attempt to justify or support the accusations contained in the song either at that time or since.)

My choices were to sue EMI for failure to receive our permission to publish the song, to sue the band for libel, or— as we were the label about to put it out—block the release of the album.

Unfortunately, events made it clear which path I had to take. Soon Freddie began to be quoted in some very nasty articles in newspapers and magazines. The articles widened his unjustified and unsupported criticisms to encompass other parts of Trident and its staff.

I had no choice. I was forced to sue EMI and the band and certain publications for a combination of libel and failure to correctly publish the product.

I had to allow the issue of the album as well, as some hundred thousand copies had been pressed without Trident's knowledge - EMI had taken their unilateral decision and the costs of scrapping the album would have a direct impact on Trident as well as the band

The issue was finally settled out of court.

Clearly Freddie's and the band's gratitude for what Trident had helped to create and achieve was non-existent. Four years of hard work by a lot of people, massive financial support seemingly meant absolutely nothing. What gratitude!

I had seen firsthand Freddie's behaviour, or as he was quoted as saying in many subsequent articles "I have created a monster, the monster is me. I have worked for this since I was a kid. I would have killed for this, it's what I have wanted, success, fame, money, sex, drugs, whatever you want."

~

The haggling over the contracts dragged on for months. The tension surrounding the negotiations got to everyone in the end. Even the coolest characters involved got hot under the collar.

There was a whole number of settlement meetings. A lot of them were just between the two solicitors, Jim Beach for the band and Ted Oldman for Trident. They were both great pros and could have tied it all up in no time. But there were too many other bruised egos involved.

For some of the meetings there needed to be a representative from each side. So that would usually be me for Trident and John Reid on behalf of the band.

I remember one day we were getting close to settling the management debt. According to the management accounts I'd produced in June, that figure was about £178,000 (c.£1.5 million). They'd agreed by now that this was how much they owed us. We'd reached a stage where we were talking about how this would be paid off. We needed to see one significant payment to clear it, we'd said. John Reid was a guy I liked. He was straightforward. At one point in the negotiations that day we agreed to take a down payment of £100,000 (c.£850,000) if we got it immediately.

"I'll write you a cheque for it now," John said, producing a chequebook from his pocket.

"We can't take it, it has to be a banker's draft," Ted told them. John Reid was always a pretty cool and composed customer. It was one of the few times I'd ever seen him hassled.

He protested, but got nowhere.

I could tell they didn't like it, but they had to accept it.

"Okay. Give us a couple of hours. We'll go and see EMI," John said.

So off they went.

A few hours later they reappeared with a banker's draft from EMI for £100,000 – ironically part of the money Trident and Queen were waiting to receive in October!

We'd been haggling for weeks over various aspects of it by then. Jim was surprised at the sums of money involved. They owed us three more albums under the contract we had. It was based on the number of tracks. They owed us three albums' worth.

Again, I just wanted to be fair. "We just want our entitlement. We'd invested on that basis," I said.

They agreed to that under a bit of duress.

They also agreed that we could keep our Trident logo on the Queen product. That would remain there until they bought us out of the publishing side, which was going to happen over a period of two years.

There was a little bit in the press during all this. Word had inevitably leaked out that things were changing on the Queen front. John Reid's arrival on the scene wasn't ever going to go unnoticed.

At some point I read somewhere that Freddie had no idea what he owed us. That really annoyed me. It was complete rubbish. We used to agree the financial position every month. And if we were going to do a tour we'd further agree with them in advance what we were going to spend. But, as I'd learned by now, that stuff just didn't register with him or the other members of the band.

~

If that was the worst of times, the best of times were still to come. When it came to releasing the first single from A Night at the Opera, the band had decided they wanted to put out something that had for a long time been referred to as "Freddie's Thing".

Freddie had begun working on this three-part, operatic piece ages ago, apparently. He'd begun building it up on his piano. The lyrics were utterly bonkers, with crazy lines like "Scaramouche, Scaramouche can you do the fandango". No one really had much of a clue what it all meant. But we knew it sounded brilliant.

Roy Thomas Baker had had a hell of a job getting it down. I heard the track and realised immediately it was extraordinary. But it was also five minutes and fifty-five seconds long. How the hell was that going to be a single, especially in a world in which stations like Radio 1 refused to play anything much over three minutes?

Fortunately, Roy Thomas Baker and the rest of us had a cunning plan. We'd had a long and happy relationship with the DJ Kenny Everett for years. I'd known him since my brief stint in management back in the mid-1960s. He was at Capital Radio at the time and was drawing huge audiences. We knew there was nothing he loved more than a bit of mischief. So we sent Roy Thomas Baker around to see him with a reel-to-reel copy of "Bohemian Rhapsody".

"You can have it to listen to but you have to promise not to play it, Kenny," he said, knowing full well what he was doing.

"Oh don't worry, I won't," Kenny said with a wink.

The next day he started playing snippets of this strange, operatic sounding record. People were soon jamming the phone lines trying to find out what it was. The more they asked the more he played it. Soon he'd played it fourteen times in just two days.

Record stores were soon being besieged by Queen fans trying to get hold of this record.

With all this fuss going on in London, a US DJ called Paul Drew at RKO also managed to lay his hands on the track. It got a similar reaction there. Again, people were asking for it in the stores. We may have been in a dispute with Elektra, but there was still no way they couldn't release this single.

We knew this was a song that needed a great video, so we'd come up with something suitably dramatic to go with it. The video opened with these images of the four boys, moving around in psychedelic circles. We'd used the same "howl around" technology on Kate Bush's single "Wuthering Heights". It was typical of what we were doing at Trilion in terms of innovation. No other company could have provided a band with this kind of thing as part of the in-house service. But there was no point trying to tell Queen that now. It was too late.

The video, the promotion, and the "guerrilla" campaign via Kenny Everett all came together perfectly. Soon "Bohemian Rhapsody" was the most played record in the country. It absolutely roared to the top of the UK charts, and stayed there for the next nine weeks. That Christmas it was by far the biggest selling record in the country.

It hit No. 9 in the US's Billboard Hot 100 as well.

Of course, it was a bittersweet moment for us. The success of "Bohemian Rhapsody" came as news was beginning to leak out to the wider world that we had split from Queen.

Around the studio there was no escaping the slight air of despondency. We'd all worked so hard to break the band. They'd been nothing more than a bunch of raw talents when they'd started using the place in the small hours of the night at the start of the 1970s. A lot of people felt a little betrayed. A few were kind enough to tell me that they felt I had been treated particularly badly.

I just shrugged my shoulders and said, to quote Mick Jagger, "It's only rock 'n' roll, and it's expensive."

That was, of course, the truth of the matter. It was only rock 'n' roll.

How many bands or artists have the same manager they started with? Very few. You saw this kind of thing all the time. The original person is the one that puts in the blood, sweat, and tears to make them what they are. And then when things take off, that's all forgotten. I was seeing the same thing on the production side of things—and the music and television sides as well. Good people would come along, you'd nurture them, and then they'd spread their wings. It was just the way it was. What could you do?

I was also realistic enough to know that I'd made mistakes. Myself and the other people involved with Queen hadn't been angels. We hadn't been involved with them for purely philanthropic purposes. We'd all been out to make them the best band we possibly could, to entertain millions of people around the world, and as a result make money—as much of it as we possibly could if we worked hard, and we all had. I'd known from the outset that they were a particularly "high maintenance" band and thought I'd got that covered.

But, for all that they liked to see themselves as artists, Queen were also ambitious young men. They too wanted to make money, and in particular, they wanted to live the rock 'n' roll lifestyle.

There was nothing wrong with that.

They failed to remember however—or maybe chose to ignore—

that it was all on account, as a business and that it would all be set against the money they made further down the road. As I dwelled on it for days, weeks, and months afterwards, I wondered whether I should somehow have made that clearer to them. They were all clever guys. The idea that they thought I was some kind of leech, as Freddie had put it, really hurt me. I hadn't been anything of the kind. I felt like rather than draining their blood, I'd been the one who'd kept it flowing.

For a while I felt a bit sorry for myself about it all. Thankfully, however, the industry rallied around me. One of the big consolations was the fact that people in the music business didn't think any different of me because of what happened. In fact, it was almost as if I'd gone through some rite of passage. I'd become part of a brotherhood of sorts.

As the news spread about the end of our relationship with Queen, I got three telegrams. One was from Peter Grant, who managed Led Zeppelin; another came from Tony Smith, who looked after Genesis; and the other—funnily enough—was from John Reid. They all said the same thing: "Sorry bout all that's happened, that's what happens. Join the club."

They'd all seen this kind of thing before. It had been part of the industry for years. And it would remain that way.

Over the years, members of Queen admitted that things could have been done differently. Brian May, in particular, said some kind things. "It was a shame," he told the BBC once. "Trident was an amazing collection of talent. If only Norman had understood that people really were unhappy. Perhaps we didn't do enough talking. We were all doing what we felt was right."

He was right, of course. We should have talked more. And I should have been more attentive to their feelings, especially early on. By the time I'd realised things were badly wrong, it was too late. By then, I think, Freddie had become a kind of monster. He was out of control. No one was going to be able to cope with his ego.

Events soon proved me right.

I had a funny feeling that John Reid wasn't actually going to stay with Freddie and Queen for that long. Sure enough, within a year or so there were rumours of trouble once more. Freddie wanted to manage himself, which was what I think he had been angling to do all along. Eventually, it would be Jim Beach who would take the reins.

The end of Freddie's relationship with John Reid was apparently even more sudden and final than the divorce from Trident.

I heard a story that was circulating around at the time that when the shit hit the fan he and John were in a limousine driving through London. They were having a row about the direction they were going in and Freddie had basically inferred that he thought John should cut his ties to them.

John was a straight talking guy and just cut to the chase.

"Okay Freddie," he said, "if you want me to leave, it will cost you a million quid". There was a child-like side to Freddie, if you challenged him he'd rise to it. That was the kind of guy he was. So Freddie got out his chequebook and wrote out a cheque for a million quid. He then got his driver to pull over at the curb and said, "Now fuck off".

John was smart enough to see that he was better off out of it. He took the money and walked off. And he didn't bother asking for a banker's draft . . .

Fourteen

Out Of The Blue

" That gesture from John, Brian, and Roger went a long way towards exorcising the ghosts of the past. "

Losing Queen had been a blow, there was no disguising it. The repercussions of the split continued for a long time, especially on the legal front as the band slowly but surely bought back all their rights from us. "In March 1977 the company finally settled with the band for the sale of all of its future rights, the rights to the old albums and the settlement of the management debt for the sum of £303,392.71(c.£1.8 million)."

As I'd promised, the royalties finally began to come online in late 1975 and 1976, and with the success of "Bohemian Rhapsody" and A Night at the Opera that income stream was soon substantial. Freddie's dream finally came true and he became a very, very wealthy man indeed, living the high life in the Kensington palace his money bought him.

Of course, he would pay a terrible price for his lifestyle, and no one was sadder to see his demise than me. He may have been a monster to deal with, but he was also a genius. And there aren't too many of those around in this world.

I did see him once, in the years following our fall out. In 1986 I took the family to Wembley to see them on the "Magic Tour". They were incredible, to me they were clearly on top of their game, we were so impressed that I arranged to go to the Knebworth concert a few weeks later, again with my family. This time I was able to meet Freddie for the first time for over 10 years. He was friendly, it was as if the rows of the past were forgotten, which helped me lay a few ghosts to rest. It was very poignant day for me; it turned out to be their last live concert. It transpired that I was at their first and last concerts.

Years later, after he had died, I went to the phenomenal Freddie Mercury Memorial Concert at Wembley. It was like Live Aid all over again; everyone from the world of rock seemed to be there. I went with the family and went backstage afterwards.

As we were walking into the hospitality area, I saw the three remaining members standing on a step being photographed. Time had healed some of the old wounds, and Brian May, in particular, had said some nice things about me and the way it had all ended. But I was still surprised—and very touched—by what happened.

As I walked by, John Deacon pointed at me and said in a loud voice so that everyone could hear him, "And if it hadn't been for that man we wouldn't be here."

Brian and Roger didn't say anything but just looked at him and then me and nodded. It was as close as they had come to saying sorry.

It was a great moment for me, especially with my family alongside. The loss of Queen had been a painful experience for me and Chris, and the kids had probably suffered indirectly through it. That gesture from John, Brian, and Roger went a long way towards exorcising the ghosts of the past.

~

As the 1970s progressed and I watched Queen go on to become one of the world's biggest rock bands, there were inevitably times when I stopped and thought about what might have been. But I knew we had to put that part of our lives behind us. After all there was plenty to be positive about as we looked to the future.

As we adjusted to a world without Queen in the Trident family, I began to realise that the work we'd done for them had left us in an incredibly strong position. No independent studio had ever invested in a band in the way we had done. And there had been huge spin-offs from the techniques and skills we'd developed on their behalf.

It had been because of Queen, for instance, that we'd first developed the idea of making videos under the wing of Trilion, our video company. When we'd started, the concept was pretty much unheard of; instead of sending promoters demo tapes and biographies why not send them a video? It had made total sense to us. And it had worked.

We had televised or worked up every single that Queen had done, right from the beginning with the "Seven Seas of Rhye" all the way through to "Bohemian Rhapsody" and would continue to do so for many more. That video really had set the cat amongst the pigeons. Almost as soon as Queen hit No. 1, the Trilion phone lines were red hot with record companies who wanted us to weave the same magic for them. We were more than happy to oblige.

As the 1970s moved on we had made videos for a whole host of artists.

Even before "Bohemian Rhapsody", Paul McCartney had remained a regular customer of ours and asked us to make a video for a single, "Jet", from the Band on the Run album he'd just made with his new group Wings, which also featured his wife Linda and Denny Laine.

We'd also done work with Genesis, The Rolling Stones, Thin Lizzy, 10cc and so many other famous artists. "Bohemian Rhapsody" really transformed things, however. Before that, a good video was a useful complement to the release of a single. After "Bohemian Rhapsody" it became a necessity. We were still a year or two away from the launch, in 1981, of MTV. But there was no doubt that this was the direction the industry was heading, and we were in the vanguard.

It was all part of the progression that had always been part of the Trident story. We were always changing with the music industry; it was a necessity.

We'd expanded our operations significantly to accommodate these new changes, and had acquired a great collection of equipment, including new OB trucks capable of capturing and transmitting live pictures. We had expanded the facilities with the acquisition of a tele-cine operation in Soho, Colour Television Consultants (CTC) who had purchased a full set of time code editing equipment from

RCA in America. It would be a first in Europe; this equipment would be a revolution in the fledgling video industry. CTC's finance arrangements had collapsed so the owner approached us; it was the natural fit to the Trilion operation. It was a system we would have acquired eventually this opportunity would save us two years, so we bought the company and all the kit from him

I merged his company with Trilion and its various companies and put them all under one roof. We acquired a lease on the De Lane Lea sound studio in Dean Street and converted it into a shooting stage complete with a car lift and full lighting rig. We had an entrance in the same street as the back of the Marquee Club, which was handy for filming live acts there.

We had some fun assignments during that time. Leo Sayer came to us to make an elaborate video for a new single . He'd had a string of big hits by then, including "When I Need You" and "The Show Must Go On".

The idea for this one was that he'd be singing in the streets of London. So we decided to use a Mole Richardson mobile crane with a four man camera boom with Leo Sayer occupying the front seat, this meant we could swing him up, down and round and round all whilst on the move, this would produce a pretty amazing video.

It was the sort of thing they did in Hollywood all the time. The difference, however, was that in Los Angeles there was room to manoeuvre a cameraman on the end of a thirty-foot boom. On the streets of London, there wasn't room to swing a cat.

We took the truck into London and started filming. We were soon clattering into lampposts and getting the truck stuck in tight streets and alleyways, much to the annoyance of the cabbies. Before we knew it, the police were pulling us to the side.

"Have you got a licence for this?" one of them asked. Of course we didn't. We were just winging it, as everyone did back then.

Television had become more and more central to our operations. I didn't see it as us moving into a new industry. I saw it more as a natural progression.

By the end of the 1970s, we even had the facilities to do live outside and studio broadcasts, which was something that brought us a lot of work with TV companies, and in particular the BBC. As we did so, we used our experience and expertise as a recording studio to revolutionise sound on television. During the late 1970s, we introduced proper audio to TV. We used the same multi-tracking systems that we used in the Trident recording studio to record music for television. It was a mark of how advanced we were that we recorded the first-ever stereo television show, a rare performance by the hugely popular German musician Bert Kaempfert from the Albert Hall. Kaempfert, who wrote the music for hits like "Strangers in the Night" and "Spanish Eyes", sold records by the truckload from the early part of the 1960 up to his death in 1980. The then-head of light entertainment at the BBC, Billy Cotton went mad for the programme we made and bought it off us.

From there we started doing all sorts of outside broadcasts. It was amazing to think about the progress we'd made. We were filming everything from Romeo and Juliet at St. George's Theatre to the Winter Olympics and World Title Boxing matches. When Pope John Paul II came to England got off the plane and kissed the ground, we were there for the BBC. These images were circulated around the world. That's how respected we were.

We covered Margaret Thatcher's opening speech when she arrived at Downing Street in 1979. We also did a lot of football matches both for the BBC's Match of the Day and for London Weekend Television.

It was a whole new business for us. Soon there were Trilion outside broadcast trucks driving all over the country.

~

We were such an integral part of the television industry that, for a brief period every Friday afternoon, we ran the ITV Network. At the time the London franchise was split between Thames TV during the week and LWT over the weekend. On Friday afternoons, one would hand over to the other. As they did so, however, there was a brief break, during which they'd air commercials. It was Trilion who put them out. For the two or three minutes it took to hand over to LWT, everyone in London and most of the southeast was in our hands. It meant that we were linked into the entire television system in the UK.

Our control centre was based in our Brewer Street offices and connected straight to the post office tower, which was then linked to the main television tower at Goonhilly in Cornwall. We could beam pictures around the world if we needed to.

~

After all the trouble with Queen, it felt great to be at the top of my game again. It also felt great to see the expression on some of my old rivals' faces when they saw what I'd been up to.

One moment I'll never forget, came when Trilion Video had been commissioned by the BBC to shoot a huge concert by Electric Light Orchestra—or ELO—at Wembley. It was a fantastic concert, full of pyrotechnics and effects. At one point a spaceship descended and opened up on stage. There were laser beams and a light show— you name it, this show had it.

One of the reasons we'd been given the gig was that we had figured out a way to shoot laser beams on TV. The BBC hadn't cracked it at the time. Nobody there had worked out how to do it, and it was too dangerous to put down to chance. If you got it wrong, you'd burn holes in the cameras. So they called us in.

I was there watching everything, and it was all going great. So midway through the concert I went back to the trucks where the control centre was to see the guys. As I picked my way through the back of the arena and out towards the trucks, who should I walk into but the familiar figure of Don Arden.

Don had been through his ups and downs like me in recent years. He'd been caught up in a legal tangle with one of his clients, the singer-songwriter Lyndsey De Paul, who claimed he'd driven her to contemplate suicide because of his non-payment of royalties. Then one of his biggest bands, Black Sabbath, sacked their lead singer Ozzy Osbourne. His daughter Sharon was, by now, dating Ozzy and—to her dad's fury—had begun managing him as well. When the pair married he cut her out of his life and didn't speak to her again for twenty years.

Around the same time the BBC's investigative reporter Roger Cook had carried out an investigation into his management methods, famously goading Don into threatening him on air. But then he struck gold with ELO, whom he'd managed because of his connection to the 1960s band The Move. As the Wembley gig tonight would underscore, ELO's blend of classic rock and catchy melodies had made them global superstars. Their albums Out of the Blue and Discovery had sold millions, making Don a rich man. On the back of their success, he'd formed his own record label, called Jet Records, and even bought Howard Hughes' old house in Beverly Hills.

So when he saw me standing there, it's fair to say he wasn't best pleased. Don being Don, he expressed his displeasure in the most straightforward language.

"What the fuck are you doing here?" he said, removing the ever-present cigar from his mouth.

"Hello Don. Long time no see," I said, adopting my normal tone with him.

"Yeah, yeah, cut out the sarcasm Norman, what are you doing at my gig?" he said.

I just smiled and turned around looking towards the giant outside broadcast truck standing behind me.

"Look at the truck," I said.

He did, but seemed nonplussed.

"Look at the logo," I said, pointing at the giant Trident symbol on the side.

"What's that got to do with you?" Don said, the colour rising in his face.

"I own it. And we're broadcasting this for the BBC," I said.

Don looked fit to burst.

"If I'd known that I'd have put a stop to it," he said. "You're the last person I'd have had doing the fucking job."

I rather enjoyed winding Don up, so I couldn't resist.

"I'll pull the plug now if you like. It's not a problem," I said, waving at one of the technicians.

Don knew full well that this was a major outside broadcast for the BBC—and for ELO.

"You fucking bastard," he said. "I'll get you."

He then turned on his fat little legs and scurried off, the usual coterie of goons waddling behind him.

I couldn't resist laughing.

Still the same old Don, I said to myself. I think that rankled with him for years afterwards, especially as the BBC aired the programme several times.

As with the recording business, the key to our success in television lay in staying ahead of the game. So we invested heavily in the latest and best equipment.

Following a working family holiday in California , I imported a giant vehicle from a company called Revcon in California. It was a real cracker. It was a thirty-four-foot motorhome, but it looked like one of the bullet-nosed 125 railway engines. It had been built on a purpose-built chassis, and was built like an aeroplane making it quite lightweight and very stable I could see this making an excellent video truck. It certainly drew glances, that's are for sure.

Around about this time Trident Records signed a deal to release Bob Marley's wife Rita's album "Who Knows It Feels It" in the UK. We decided to take her on a promo tour around the various radio stations using my motorhome.

We took it along to Capital Radio, where it immediately drew admiring looks. Within a couple of days, I fielded a call from one of the main technical guys there asking me where I'd gotten it. I told them a bit about it.

"Do you reckon you could design one of those to be a radio studio?" he asked. "We were thinking that we could start doing mobile radio broadcasts from it."

"Sure," I said.

I got on to Revcon over in the States and I was soon designing this thing for them. I had the bodywork modified over in the US. It had big windows on the side and rear, the interior included a seating area, a driving area, and even a kitchen. That left us to install the interior. At the back it had a whole area devoted to this mobile radio studio. It even had its own generator on board. It would be able to transmit and broadcast from pretty much anywhere, we reckoned.

Before we could hand it over to Capital, it needed fitting out, which we were going to carry out in conjunction with the Capital engineers. We completed the work and were within a day or so of delivering it to Capital when events took an unexpected turn. I'd taken charge of the vehicle and had driven it out to a weighbridge in Ware Hertfordshire. We needed to get its specifications registered for insurance and licensing purposes.

I was in the cab of the truck on the weighbridge when suddenly all of the communications lit up. There was an urgent telephone call.

It was the Capital Radio office back in London.

"What's up?" I said.

"There's an emergency. There's been a giant fire at Alexandra Palace and Capital are off the air. They want to use the truck now to broadcast. They also want to use your other one."

I rang my brother-in-law and asked him to take the other Revcon into town. It was parked at my house at the time.

I was halfway to Alexandra Palace when I got a message through on the CB radio system.

"There's been a change of plan. Nicky Horne is going to do a live broadcast from the South Bank. Can you meet him there?"

I drove through West London in this giant vehicle, a thousand thoughts racing through my head.

We hadn't really pre-tested the rig properly. We had carried out some tests but we didn't know if it was going to work in a full broadcast scenario. What if it didn't? Would Capital hand the thing back saying it was useless? I got to the South Bank, where I parked it up, got it stabilised, and set the generator running. I checked for a radio signal. It was great. It was coming through loud and clear. Nicky Horne turned up with an engineer and a pile of records, looking flustered.

"Hope this works," Nicky said.

"So do I," I said. The engineer got into the mobile studio and was soon giving me the thumbs up.

"Perfect," he said. "Nicky Horne stayed on air for two hours that evening."

The truck soon became a real attraction for Capital. It was even invited to be part of the procession in that year's Lord Mayor's Show. No one else fancied driving it through the narrow streets of the city. So I agreed to do it for them. I loved it.

It was fairly typical of day-to-day life during that phase of the Trident story. Running a string of companies was never easy—or dull. At one stage we had acquired a company called Liveware to provide and rig PA systems for all of our artists. Late one night I got a phone call from the police informing me they'd found one of our trucks on Hackney Marshes—full of musical instruments.

"Well, there's nothing odd in that," I said.

"But these are all brand new instruments, Mr. Sheffield," the officer said.

It turned out that a member of the Liveware road crew had "lent" the truck to a mate. This mate had used it to rob the CBS instrument warehouse in London.

Of course, it all turned into another drama for me to sort out, and we had to bring charges against everyone involved. As I said, there was never a dull moment.

~

The upshot of all this success was that our reputation was spreading far beyond the UK. We were getting a lot of enquiries from the States about our video division. I had sensed that it was presenting an opportunity for us, so I'd been in negotiation to merge our operations in the US with a studio in Los Angeles called The Record Plant.

It was, in many ways, the Trident of the States.

The studio had been formed by a couple of guys: a sales executive called Chris Stone and a brilliant sound engineer and studio designer called Gary Kellgren. Gary had worked at the famous Brill building in New York, churning out a conveyor belt of hits in the 1960s. Just like EMI in England, the Brill building was a cold place. Gary once described the studios there as "sterile, utilitarian places" where "engineers wore jackets and ties". Instead, he wanted to build an environment which encouraged artists to relax and be creative. They had begun their business with an innovative and very different studio on West 44th Street in New York. The place was acoustically amazing—and it came complete with a living room where people could create and a Jacuzzi to relax. Needless to say, artists had fallen in love with it. One of the first to record there was Frank Zappa. Jimi Hendrix and The Velvet Underground soon followed. Encouraged by this success, they'd opened a second studio in Los Angeles. That had then expanded into another studio in Sausalito.

Like Trident, The Record Plant had really taken off when one of The Beatles had recorded there. In their case it was John Lennon, who made Imagine with them in 1971. Since then they'd recorded artists from Aerosmith and Sly and the Family Stone to the Eagles and Fleetwood Mac. The albums recorded there were among the most successful of the 1970s; among them were Born to Run by Bruce Springsteen, Rumours by Fleetwood Mac, Hotel California by The Eagles, and Songs in the Key of Life by Stevie Wonder. A lot of the artists who used Trident had also used The Record Plant, so we'd forged a bit of a relationship.

Around the time the whole Queen situation was coming to a head, I'd started talking to Chris Stone about the possibility of a merger. He and Gary Kellgren had been up for it. Financially, strategically, and creatively it made massive sense, for both of us. Chris and Gary wanted to tap into Trident's video expertise as well as our experience in music recording. They wanted us to build a video operation on the site of the LA studio. Record Plant were very big in mobile audio they had recorded Wood Stock, there was a huge opportunity. As far as we could tell, there was only one independent outside broadcast unit in Los Angeles, and the music video industry was a couple of years behind the UK in terms of the technology and techniques they were using. I was incredibly excited about it. And in the wake of us severing our links with Queen, I thought it was the perfect way to bounce back, as it were. A Trident/Record Plant merger would dominate the music business. It seemed like the deal of a lifetime.

So we agreed to step up the process; we had the LA premises surveyed, and began drawing up contracts for a deal. In the meantime, I also persuaded Chris to come and spend some time over in California with the children. We rented a house in Beverly Hills and got a taste for the life out there. The kids loved it, needless to say. Chris too thought we could make a go of it over there, although she was concerned about the education system. It looked like we were heading west to California. Unfortunately, there was to be a twist in the tale.

~

Our success wasn't just attracting interest in the States. We had fans in other parts of the world as well. And nowhere were we in more demand than in South Africa.

We'd first been approached in the mid-1970s by a couple of South African businessmen who wanted us to do something that was deeply illegal. They'd asked us whether we could make copies of the master tapes of football matches that we'd filmed for London Weekend Television and the BBC's Match of the Day.

I remember at the time thinking they were insane. We were only one of two companies in the UK to cover football matches for the ITV and BBC. If we did that we'd have killed Trilion Video business stone dead. It would have been suicide. So we told them not to be stupid.

A little while later, however, they'd come back. This time they asked us whether we'd be interested in building a video facility to compliment their video duplication plant out in Johannesburg. They were also talking about building a full-blown video facility. There was no doubt they had a lot of money. We checked the guys out—one was Jewish, the other an Afrikaan—and they had substantial business interests in South Africa. They also had the backing of the official state television company, SABC, the South African Broadcasting Corporation.

I felt uncomfortable about working in South Africa from the beginning. You have to remember that this was the 1970s and apartheid was still at its height. Doing business with South Africa was fraught with problems. A lot of it was illegal. Mandela was still in jail, and there were riots going on in places like Soweto and Sharpville. The whole situation out there was horrible.

But there was no doubting the fact that they wanted to do business with us. We formed a joint company, Trilion S.A. Soon they'd got a large bank to finance the building of the video facility. We had to design the facility and provide the bulk of the staff, while they would supply the equipment. We also supplied an outside broadcast truck. Soon, we were up and running.

For a while, I and other members of the Trilion board was going back and forth to Johannesburg like a yo-yos, working mad hours putting everything together. The station was soon broadcasting.

With the blessing of the SABC, they asked us to video black football matches. Home based crews couldn't do it because of apartheid. I'll never forget, the first game we shot in Soweto, the match was between a black team and a white team. The black team won it easily, which made me smile.

As things clicked into place, we were soon branching into commercials out there. There was a lot of money flying around but the South African television audience was very small compared to the UK at that time so it wasn't exactly the centre of the creative universe. And it was also, frankly, a very unpleasant place to be living at that time in its history. I really didn't like it. Besides, my heart—and my head—was telling me to focus my energies on Los Angeles.

As I'd begun putting together the deal with Record Plant in Los

Angeles, I'd kind of handed the keys to the South African operation over to our staff there. My brother Barry, who was very keen on what we were doing in Africa was left holding the baby.

Unfortunately, like all babies, it was soon proving extremely demanding. Almost immediately after we got involved in the South African deal, we found our finances being stretched to the limit.

At the time, I'd agreed to go ahead with investing in the video facility in Jo'burg, I hadn't anticipated it would have such an impact on us.

The problem was that we were now beginning to get stretched on all fronts.

Very quickly, I began to realise that we had to make some big decisions. Realistically, we couldn't expand our operation in South Africa and invest in the US at the same time. We had to concentrate on one or the other. There were now four of us on the board of the main company, myself, Barry, our two investors, alongside Trilion's MD Bill Hope. I told them that we had to sit down and have a talk about what was happening. We had to make a choice.

We started getting together all the information we needed to make a decision. We had good, hard data on the American situation. The size of the market and the potential earnings there were pretty clear to see. South Africa was a different thing, however. The potential income figures there were just speculation. We had no real idea what it would earn us. In theory it could be a goldmine. But it could also be a dud—we were working in a very small market at that time, after all.

I was the chairman of the company and—to my mind—it was an absolute no brainer. The merger with Record Plant was going to turn us into a powerhouse. We'd get a foothold in the States. And we'd be able to expand and diversify our business into a huge market.

There were all sorts of options. At that point, we still had the rights to some of Queen's material. We could do well with that over there. Our old sound engineer Malcolm Toft had also been running a business with us selling the Trident mixing desks, which was going great guns in the USA. People everywhere wanted desks that had the Trident capabilities. With that incorporated into the American operation as well, I was convinced we'd make a bomb.

By contrast, the South African operation was a pain in the butt. It was already draining money at a prodigious rate. I was also deeply uncomfortable about the whole apartheid thing. A lot of our clients had artists who were black or politically opposed to apartheid. How were they going to react to us being a big noise in South Africa? Not very well I suspected.

So, to me, it was cut and dried. It was simple—we'd throw all our resources into America and knock South Africa on the head.

When it came to the board meeting, however, I discovered that the other guys didn't see it quite the same way.

Barry, in particular, was very money motivated at that point in his life. He had got a taste for the high life and he wanted more of it. He had somehow decided that we were going to make our fortunes out in South Africa. He also had misgivings about the merger with Record Plant for some reason that I didn't really understand.

Unsurprisingly, the money aspect of the equation was what interested the other two board members the most. They weren't creative people. They were businessmen. The bottom line was all that interested them. However, I had a good relationship with Bill Hope, having worked very closely with him for many years. I spent time explaining the pros and cons to him. He seemed to see what I was getting at.

As the meeting went on, however, I began to get a funny, sinking feeling in my stomach. The others seemed to be buying into the idea that South Africa was where the really big money was to be made.

At the same time, they were coming up with all sorts of negatives about the deal with Record Plant. I dealt with every one of them, knocking down their arguments each time. But it didn't seem to make much difference.

"I don't believe this," I kept saying to myself through the meeting.

Sure enough, when it got to a vote, I'd been screwed. I had hoped that Bill Hope would back me. A two-two split would have given me, as chairman, the casting vote and I'd have given the Record

Plant deal the nod. But he voted with the other two. Unbelievable.

I thought they had taken leave of their senses, so I told them I thought they were all absolutely mad.

I had to tell Chris Stone of Record Plant that the deal was off. That was hard enough, but then I had to break it to Chris and the kids that we weren't going to live in Beverly Hills after all. They were really upset.

At the time, I think, I had been naïve. I'd been so focussed on the nuts and bolts of putting the American deal together that it hadn't occurred to me that I'd face opposition at board level. They had all been in favour for many months. To be honest, it hadn't crossed my mind that launching a video studio in South Africa would be a more attractive proposition than becoming a major player in the most important music and television market in the world.

Looking back on it now, I can see that it was a huge turning point. Trident—and I—had reached a crossroads. We were heading in different directions. And we would both soon be reaching our journey's end . . .

Fifteen

Full Circle

"What is it? he asked. A piece of history."

As I walked through the streets of Soho one grey morning in the Autumn of 1981, all sorts of memories were flashing through my head. Passing by an office block I saw a young man running out clutching a brown parcel, looking like he had to get it somewhere in a real hurry. That took my mind back to the day I received Marc Bolan's "special delivery" and I'd had to run over to Savile Row to dispose of it.

Walking by a Ronnie selling fresh flowers in Brewer street market, I remembered Old Rose, the old boy who used to wear a flower behind his ear. He'd passed away many years back, as had so many of the old characters. The place felt a little bit empty without them.

Of course, Soho was still the epicentre of the entertainment business in London, perhaps more so than ever. I had a bit of time to kill, so I walked past a couple of the pubs that were its heartbeat, the French House, where all the actors and journos hung out, the Fox & Blue Posts where the film crews had a pint, and, of course, The Ship, where the music industry still gathered for a good old gossip.

It was weird walking past them all, knowing that I was no longer a part of the community and that—once I'd got today's little errand out of the way—I was unlikely to pass by this way again. I was heading to the old Trident studios for the very last time.

~

In the space of two years, between 1979 and 1981, The Trident Group had fallen apart. What had been a thriving, multi-faceted business had become a pale shadow of its former self. Just as I'd suspected, it had been the decision to focus on South Africa rather than America that had been our undoing.

The move had been every bit as misguided as I had predicted. Barry and the other board members had seen nothing but dollar signs. But there was no way it was ever going to be that easy in a country like that, with all its political and logistical problems. Sure enough, the cost of keeping an operation going out there had soon been eating up money at a ferocious rate. We were soon sending £50,000 (c.£240,000) a month out. It was madness. Barry was forced to head out there to take over the day-to-day running of the operation. We were also forced to start breaking up the Trident operation here in the UK.

The first thing we'd divested ourselves of had been our tape duplication plant, which we'd sold to our main competitor. That actually made perfect business sense. We had been going head to head with this company for years and we were just undercutting each other by a penny each time. The only beneficiaries were our clients: RCA, EMI, and the other labels. I had approached them with view to buying their company, but they in turn offered us a bigger sum to sell Trident Tape Services to them.

We got a very good price for the business. It had been a very good source of income to the Trident companies during its time, but such were the demands of the African operation that the proceeds were soon being poured down there.

Reinvesting in Trident's other core businesses—the studio and the London video company—wasn't an option, especially as the former was experiencing difficulties. Business wasn't as lively as it had been in the glory days of the late sixties and early seventies. As the 1970s had drawn to a close and the 1980s had begun, there had been a subtle but significant shift in the music industry and the way it worked. Punk had changed things a lot, musically speaking. Electronic music too had come to the fore. For obvious reasons, a lot of music was being recorded in a different way, by a new generation of musicians. During 1979 we had recorded Charlie, Phoenix, Bill Bruford, Brand X, B.T.O., Aex Costandino, Rush, Tina Turner, and many others. In 1980 things changed with a recession on as well, so the recording studio side of the business had taken a bit of a dip. There had been budget cutbacks by the record labels, and many of the electronic bands were recording at home. This left us with a lot of disco-type work at low rates.

We were still getting people in there. Generation X had been one of the new wave acts who'd recorded with us. And Canadian bands like Rush still liked to come to Trident. But now we were falling further and further behind in terms of technology. It was ironic that Trident, the studio that had once led the world, was now lagging behind tiny little operations in obscure little places. The digital world was beginning, and we weren't involved.

So with South Africa draining our resources, the other three members of the board began making noises about closing the studio down. I was flabbergasted. Trident was the bedrock of our business. It was what had got us where we were today, it was also my baby. I couldn't contemplate selling it, Trilion was going to need it in the not too distant future.

The negotiations were long and protracted, but eventually we came up with a plan. I offered the rest of the board a deal. I said that I would sell enough shares back to them so that I had enough money to purchase and run the studio as a separate entity. When I got it back up and running profitably, they would buy back the shares and they could bring the company back under the Trident Group umbrella, as it were. As part of the deal I would I would receive all of the assents and the staff along with the ownership of the Trident name and the Trident Logo.

They agreed in principle, although the value of my shares exceeded the value of the studio, Bill Hope suggested that we did a deal in which they paid the balance due me in two tranches. Foolishly, I agreed. I got the first chunk and in 1981 began working at the studio. But then, it became clear that I wasn't going to get the second chunk of money from the other directors. I had arranged bank funds to match my input, and that would have allowed the studio to begin upgrading itself and continue its work.

Slowly but surely, it dawned on me what was happening. They were going to choke the life out of the studio. By late 1981, I was waving the white flag. The bookings had begun to dry up and we were struggling to pay the wages.

When we'd moved in there in 1967, we had signed a seventeen-year lease.

In 1981 we had done fourteen years. There were two-and-a-half years to go. I decided to sell the studio while it was still worth something.

In December 1981 I sold the studio to our French agent John Phillipe Illiesco, Rusty Egan, and one of our engineers Steve Short, and their backers. There was a very tearful goodbye drink with all of the crew.

~

At that point Barry and I fell out. My brother and I had always been close. I had after all, brought him into the industry, we'd started the whole thing together and, wrongly, I'd assumed we'd end it together. Unfortunately he had very different ideas about how to dispose of things than I did. I didn't expect him to side with Michael Jardine-Paterson. It came down to another vote. His memorable line to me, was, "I'm not backing you, I'm not backing Bill, I'm backing the money." In other words, he was going to do what Michael Jardine-Paterson wanted to do, both me and Trident could go to hell. Which, as it turned out, we did. They even contrived to remove me as group Chairman and as a director of all of the Trident /Trilion companies – that I had started - in my absence.

It eventually got legal and became very nasty.

I fought them in court but wasted £25,000 getting nowhere, of course my bills were paid personally and theirs were corporate. They finally settled in November 1983. In the meantime Chris and I had to sell our house. It was a horrendous time in my life. The shock of having to sue my brother was worse than anything. What had happened to family loyalty? We had worked together successfully over fifteen years. Just to rub salt into the wound, within weeks of me selling Trident Studios Barry opened an audio suite at the Trilion building just around the corner!

The new owners ran Trident for five more years until they in turn sold it on to another ex-Trident engineer. They also ran it for a number of years, until 1990. In September 1983 Barry and the others finally shook off the South African business. Trilion just became a UK television company, which they floated on the market to get themselves out of trouble. They took a financial bath in real terms. They'd had five years of murder down there. It had been a pointless exercise. If we'd gone to America we'd have had a field day and who knows what could have happened?

~

Prior to the hand-over to the new owners, there was one last job to be done, and that was to clear the tape library.

And so it was that I was heading to the Trident studio for the last time.

My son Darren and an ex-tape op came with me. They were going to help me and sort everything out. We went up to the tape library and started to move all of our clients' tapes on to the second floor, which was empty, and group everything into record or production companies, then we could contact them and get them to collect their product.

God, there was an awful lot of tapes.

It was amazing to think that the companies had left masters going back years with us. We had log sheets from the library, and of course every box had a label showing all of the data we needed: date, artist, producer, recording format, etc. It took Darren and me several days to complete this task, and it was amazing what we found. After a lot of phone calls and cab runs, I was amazed at how many companies didn't seem to be bothered. I ran ads in all the music press giving a deadline for collection, otherwise those uncollected tapes would go to a security company in Central London and they would have to pick them up from there.

As we were getting to the end of the pile I turned a box over and noticed the label on it. "Bloody hell," I said this time out loud. It was the master of the stereo mix for "Hey Jude"! EMI had never collected it, because the single was released in mono.

For a moment or two I just stood there, lost in my thoughts. My mind went back to those crazy couple of days when The Beatles had rolled into St. Anne's Court. I remembered Paul and the Orchestra, Ringo sneaking back into the studio. Most of all I remembered the expressions on Paul, John, and George Martin's faces when we'd played the recording back to them at full volume. That would live with me forever, I knew.

As I stood there lost in my thoughts, it suddenly struck me: we'd come full circle. The Trident story was ending where it had begun. It had been "Hey Jude" that had really put us on the musical map. The Beatles had introduced us to the world—and for the next decade and a half the world had come along to the little alleyway in Soho.

For a minute or two I sat on a windowsill on my own. Holding the master tape in my hands randomly, my mind ran through the myriad of events that had unfolded here inside this ordinary-looking building.

We'd welcomed some of the most amazing and talented artists of their age. We'd helped them to create the soundtrack of the late sixties and the seventies. The list of songs and albums that had been recorded in our studio still reads like an A to Z of British musical history of the era: The White Album, Space Oddity, Goodbye Yellow Brick Road, Sheer Heart Attack. They'd all been born in this building. So too, of course, had our biggest success story, Queen. They'd probably spent more hours inside this building than any other musicians, twiddling and tweaking their sound in the small hours while they were our house band. Bless them, "The Queenies".

But now those days were over.

Everything was laid out to be collected.

"That's the lot," Darren said.

"Apart from this one," I said, waving The Beatles' master at him.

I had packaged the tape up and put Apple's address on it.

"I think you should take it there by hand," I said. "It's only a few blocks away."

"What is it?" he asked.

"A piece of history."

I then told Darren what it was. He looked as white as a sheet as he took off. I told him I would meet him at The Ship as I followed him out of the door. The chill in the air and the grey clouds overhead only added to the mood: it was a sad day, a bittersweet moment. As I turned out of the alley, past the entrance to The Ship and down Wardour Street for the last time, I felt a mixture of sadness, nostalgia, regret but—above all—pride.

I still feel all those things to this day . . .

D I S C O G R A P H Y

An Interactive Version of this discography is also available at LifeonTwoLegs.com

ALBUMS RECORDED, MIXED OR CONTRIBUTED TO BETWEEN 1968 - 1981

Beatles	White Album	1968
Bee Gees	Odessa	1968
Black Sabbath	Black Sabbath	1968
Harold McNair	Harold McNair Quartet	1968
James Taylor	James Taylor	1968
Manfred Mann:	My Name is Jack	1968
Sweet Thursday	Sweet Thursday	1968
The Black Dyke Mills Band	Thingamebob	1968
The Small Faces	Ogdons Nut Gone Flake	1968
Tyrannosaurus Rex	Prophets, Seers & Sages	1968
Tyrannosaurus Rex	Unicorn	1968
Aphrodite's Child	It's Five O'Clock	1969
Bakerloo	Bakerloo	1969
Beatles	Abbey Road	1969
Billy Preston	That The Way God Planned It	1969
Bonzo Dog Band	Keynsham	1969
Bonzo Dog Band	Tadpoles	1969
David Bowie	Space Oddity	1969
Doris Troy	Aint That Cute	1969
Egg	Egg	1969
Idle Race	Idle Race	1969
Jackie Lomax	Is This What You Want	1969
Joe Cocker	With a Littels Help From my Friends	1969
Marsh Hunt	Walk on GuildedSplinters	1969
Michael Chapman	Rainmaker	1969
Rare Bird	Rare Bird	1969
Plastic Ono Band	Cold Turkey	1969
Stawbs	Dragonfly	1969
Tea and Symphony	Asylum For The Musically Insane	1969
The Jeff Beck Group	Beck-Ola (Re-master Version)	1969
The Nice	Nice	1969
Tyrannosaurus Rex	A Beard Of Stars	1969
Van Der Graaf Gen.	The Least We Can Do Is Wave To Each Other	1969
Van Der Graaf Gen.	The Aerosol Grey Machine	1969
Yes	Yes	1969
Andwella	World's End	1970
Bad Finger	Is That What You Want	1970
Black Widow	Sacrifice	1970
Blodwyn Pig	Getting To This	1970
Brian Davison	Every Which Way	1970
David Bowie	The Man Who Sold The World	1970
David Lewis	Songs Of David Lewis	1970
Elton John	Elton John	1970
Elton John	Friends OST	1970
Elton John	Tumbleweed Connection	1970
Free	Fire And Water	1970
Genesis	Trespass	1970

Genesis	The Hiding Place	1970
Gentle Giant	Gentle Giant	1970
George Harrison	All Things Must Pass	1970
Hawkwind	Hawkwind	1970
Jade	Fly On Strangewings	1970
Leonard Cohen	Songs Of Love And Hate	1970
Lindisfarne	Nicely Out Of Tune	1970
Magna Carta	Seasons	1970
May Blitz	May Blitz	1970
Michael Chapman	Window	1970
Necleus	Elastic Rock	1970
Rolling Stones	Get Yer Ya-Yas Out	1970
Shawn Phillips	Contribution	1970
T Rex	T Rex	1970
The Nice	5 Bridges	1970
Trevor Billmuss	Family Apology	1970
Van Der Graaf Gen.	H to He, Who Am The Only One	1970
Al Stewart	Orange	1971
America	America	1971
Andwella	Peoples People	1971
Audience	Lunch	1971
Audience	House on the Hill	1971
Buddy Bohn	A Drop In The Ocean	1971
Catherine Howe	What a Beautiful Place	1971
Colin Scot	Colin Scot	1971
David Bowie	Ziggy Stardust	1971
David Bowie	Hunky Dory	1971
Dr John	The Sun, Moon and Herbs	1971
Elton John	Madman Across the Water	1971
Elton John	11-17-70	1971
Gasolin'	Gasolin'	1971
Genesis	Nursery Cryme	1971
Harry Nilsson	Nillson Schilsson	1971
Indian Summer	Indian Summer	1971
John Entwistle	Smash Your Head Against The Wall	1971
Keef Hartley Band	Overdog	1971
Lindisfarne	Fog on the Tyne	1971
Lou Reed	Transformer	1971
Magna Carta	Songs From Wasties Orchard	1971
Mary Hopkin	Earth Song/Ocean Song	1971
Miller Anderson	Bright City	1971
Nazareth	Nazareth	1971
Peter Hammill	Fool's Mate	1971
Queen	Queen	1971
Ralph McTell	You Well Meaning Brought Me Here	1971
Rolling Stones	Sticky Fingers	1971
Shawn Phillips	Second Contribution	1971
Spring	Spring	1971
T Rex	Electric Warrior	1971
The Nice	Elegy	1971

Paul Williams	In Memory of Robert Johnson	1971
Van Der Graaf Gen.	Pawn Hearts	1971
Affinty	Affinity	1972
America	Homecoming	1972
Atomic Rooster	Made In England	1972
Byzantium	Byzantium	1972
Carly Simon	No Secrets	1972
Cass Elliot	Road Is No Place For A Lady	1972
Chris Money	I'm Sitting Here	1972
David Bowie	Aladdin Sane	1972
Elton John	Honky Chateau	1972
Elton John	Don't Shoot Me...	1972
Fishbaugh, and Zorn	F, F and Z	1972
Harry Nilsson	Son Of Schmilsson	1972
Home	Home	1972
Jackson Heights	The Fith Avenue Bus	1972
Joan Armatrading	Whatever's For Us	1972
Larry Lurex (Freddie Mercury)	I Can Hear Music	1972
Mahavishnu Orch.	Birds Of Fire	1972
Mike D'Arbo	Down at Rachel's Place	1972
Mott The Hoople	All The Young Dudes	1972
Nazareth	Exercises	1972
Pilot	Pilot	1972
Rick Wakeman	The Six Wives Of Henry VIII	1972
Samuel Prody	Samuel Prody	1972
Savoy Brown	Hellbound Train	1972
Savoy Brown	Lions Share	1972
Shawn Phillips	Faces	1972
Shawn Phillips	Collaboration	1972
Ace	Five-a-Side	1973
Al Stewart	Past Present and Future	1973
Alan Hull (Lindisfarne)	Pipe Dream	1973
Billy Cobham:	Spectrum	1973
Blood Sweat and Tears	No Sweat	1973
Captain Beyond	Sufficiently Breathless	1973
Chi Coltrane	Let It Ride	1973
David Bowie	Pinups	1973
Dana Gillespie	Weren't Born A Man	1973
Elton John	Goodbye Yellow Brick Road	1973
Frank Zappa	Chungas Revenge	1973
Gypsy	Brenda And The Rattlesnake	1973
Home	The Alchemest	1973
Jonathan Kelly	Wait Till They Change The Backdrop	1973
Julien Clerc	Julien	1973
Lindisfarne	Roll On Ruby	1973
Mahavishnu Orch.	The Lost Trident Sessions	1973
Peter Hammill	Chameleon In The Shadow Of The Night	1973
Peter Hammill	The Silent Corner And The Empty Stage	1973
Philip Goodhand Tate	Philip Goodhand Tate	1973
Queen	Queen II	1973

Ace	Time For Another	1974
Baker Gurvitz Army	Baker Gurvitz Army	1974
Barclay James Harvest	Everyone Is Everyone Else	1974
Billy Cobham	Crosswinds	1974
Chris De Burgh	Far Beyond These Castle Walls	1974
Elton John	Caribou	1974
Elton John	Captain Fantastic...	1974
Fats Domino	Live at Montreux	1974
Ferris Wheel	Ferris Wheel	1974
Ian Thomas	Long Long Way	1974
Jerry Goodman/Jan Hammer	Like Children	1974
Linda Ronstadt	Heart Like aWheel	1974
Lou Reed	Sally Can't Dance	1974
Love	Reel To Real	1974
Mahavishnu Orch.	Visions Of An Emerald Beyond	1974
Man	Rhinos,Winos,And Lunatics	1974
Mick Ronson	Slaughter on 10th Ave	1974
Mick Ronson	Play Don't Worry	1974
Peter Hammill	Nadir's Big Chance	1974
Peter Hammill VDGG	In Camera	1974
Queen	Sheer Heart Attack	1974
Supertramp	Crime of the Century	1974
Thin Lizzy	Nightlife	1974
Baker Gurvitz Army	Elysian Encounter	1975
Brand X	Unorthodox Behavior	1975
Brian Auger's Oblivion Express	Reinforcements	1975
Brian Eno	Heat Treatment	1975
Eddie Howell	Gramaphone Record	1975
Esperanto	Rock Orchestra	1975
Genesis	A Trick Of The Tail	1975
Isotope	Deep End	1975
Kai Olsson	Once in A While	1975
Lenny White	Venusian Summer	1975
Nutz	Nutz Too	1975
Tommy Bolin	Teaser	1975
Billy Cobham	Live On Tour In Europe	1976
Black Oak Arkansas '	10 Yr Overnight Success	1976
Brand X	Moroccan Roll	1976
Cerrone	Love In C Minor	1976
Charlie	Fantasy Girls	1976
Curved Air	Airborne	1976
Genesis	Wind and Wuthering	1976
Gong	Gazuese	1976
Graham Parker &Rumour	Discreet Music	1976
Halfbreed	Halfbreed	1976
Jack Lancaster/ Robin Lumley	Marscape	1976
Jack Lancaster/ Robin Lumley	Peter and The Wolf	1976
Jeff Beck	Wired	1976
Judge Dread	The Last Of The Skinheads	1976
Mahavishnu Orchestra	Inner Worlds	1976

Narada Michael Walden	Garden Of Love Light	1976
Nova	Vimana	1976
Peter Tosh	Legalize It	1976
Phoenix	Phoenix	1976
Return To Forever	Romantic Warrior	1976
Shakti w. John McLaughlin	A Handful Of Beauty	1976
Spiders From Mars	Spiders From Mars	1976
Tommy Bolin	Private Eyes	1976
Veronique Sanson	Vancouver	1976
West African Cosmos	W. A. C. Et Umban U Kset	1976
Alain Chamfort	Rock n Rose	1977
Alphonso Johnson	Spellbound	1977
Anthony Phillips	Wise After The Event	1977
Bill Bruford	Feels Good To Me	1977
Brand X	Livestock	1977
Café Jacques	Round The Back	1977
Cerrrone	Cerrone 3: Supernature	1977
Charlie	No Second Chance	1977
City Boy	Young Men Gone West	1977
City Boy	Dinner At The Ritz	1977
Clover	Unavailable	1977
Don Ray	The Garden Of Love	1977
Genesis	Seconds Out	1977
Genesis	And Then There Were Three	1977
John Kongas	Africanism	1977
Kayak	Starlight Dancer	1977
Love and Kisses	Love and Kisses	1977
Nova	Wings of Love	1977
Pat Travers	Putting It Straight	1977
Quantum Jump	Barracuda	1977
Radiator	Isn't It Strange	1977
Revelacion	The House Of The Rising Sun	1977
Sphinx	Sphinx	1977
Stomu Yamashta's Go	Go Too	1977
Sumeria	Golden Tears	1977
U.K.	U.K.	1977
Voyage	Voyage	1977
Warsaw Pakt	Needle Time	1977
Theo Vaness	Back To Music	1978
Alec R Costandinos	Trocadero Lemon Blue	1978
Alec R Costandinos and Syn. Orch.	Hunchback Of Notre Dame	1978
Alec R Costandinos and Syn. Orch.	Romeo and Juliet	1978
Anthony Phillips	Sides	1978
Brand X	Masques	1978
Cerrone	Bridage Montaine OST	1978
Cerrone	Cerrone 4: The Golden Touch	1978
Chantal Curtis	Get Another Love	1978
Charlie	Lines	1978
Chi Chi Favelas	Rock Solid	1978
City Boy	Book Early	1978

Lonnie Donegan	Putting on The Style	1978
Gene Simmons	Gene Simmons	1978
Jack Bruce	Jet Set Jewel	1978
John McLaughlin	Electric Guitarist	1978
Judas Priest	Rocka Rolla	1978
Kayak	Phantom Of The Opera	1978
Kikrokos	Jungle DJ & Dirty Kate	1978
Love And Kisses	How Much, How Much I Love You	1978
Michael Stanley Band	Cabin Fever	1978
Micheal Zager Band	Lifes a Party	1978
Miquel Brown	Symphony Of Love	1978
Pado & Co	Pado & Co	1978
Paris Connection	Paris Connection	1978
Paul Stanley	Paul Stanley	1978
Peter Gabriel	2	1978
Rod Argent	Moving Home	1978
Renaissance	A Song For All Seasons	1978
Revelacion	Don't Give A Damn	1978
Rush	Hemispheres	1978
Saint Tropez	Belle De Jour	1978
Sunshine on The world	Sunshine on The world	1978
Voyage	Fly Away	1978
Alec R Costandinos	Winds Of Change	1979
Alex R Costandinos	Synergy	1979
Aviator	Aviator	1979
B.T.O.	Rock n' Roll Nights	1979
Bill Bruford	One Of A Kind	1979
Brand X	Do They Hurt?	1979
Brand X	Product	1979
Brand X	Is There Anything About?	1979
Chantereau/Dahan/Pezin	Disco & Co	1979
Chantereau/Dahan/Pezin	Disco & Co Vol. 2	1979
Charlie	Fight Dirty	1979
Cowboys International	The Original Sin	1979
Croisette	Keep It On Ice	1979
Difference	High Fly	1979
Eastbound Expressway	Eastbound Expressway	1979
Evelyn Thomas	Have A Little Faith In Me	1979
Frantique	Frantique	1979
Ironhorse	Ironhouse	1979
Jack Lancaster/ Rick Van Der Linden	Wild Connections	1979
James Wells	Explosion	1979
Karen Cheryl	Liars Beware	1979
La Velle	Right Now	1979
Love De-Luxe	Again and Again	1979
Mellrose	Mellrose	1979
Random Hold	Random Hold	1979
Random Hold	Etceteraville	1979
Real Thing	Saints Or Sinners	1979
Demis Roussos	Universum	1979

Rush	Permanent Waves	1979
Sauveur Mallia	Spatial & Co	1979
Sean Delaney	Highway	1979
Seventh Avenue	Midnight In Manhattan	1979
Sylvia Mason	Sylvia Mason	1979
Tina Turner	Love Explosion	1979
Wooderoffe/Greenslade	The Pentateuch Of The Cosmogny	1979
Writz	Writz	1979
Cerrone	Cerrone 5: Angelina	1980
Cerrone	Cerrone VI	1980
Charlie	Here Comes Trouble	1980
Jimmy Pursey `	Imagination Camouflage	1980
Krisma	Cathode Mamma	1980
Magazine (H. Devoto)	Play	1980
Mental As Anything	Expresso Bongo	1980
Random Hold	The View From Here	1980
Samson	Head On	1980
The Bloodied Sword	The Bloodied Sword	1980
Vladimir Cosma	La Boum OST	1980
Jimmy Pursey	Alien Orphan	1981
Magazine (H. Devoto)	Murder And The Weather	1981
Spandau Ballet	Journeys To Glory	1981
The Wanderers	Only Lovers Left Alive	1981
Tygers Of Pan Tang	Crazy Nights	1981

SINGLES RECORDED, MIXED OR CONTRIBUTED TO BETWEEN 1968 - 1981.

Arthur Brown	Fire	1968
The Beatles	Hey Jude	1968
Bonzo Dog Do Da Band	Urban spaceman	1968
Manfred Mann	My name is Jack	1968
Mary Hopkins	Those were the days	1968
T Rex	Debora	1968
Bad Company	Come and get it	1969
Billy Preston	That's the way	1969
David Bowie	Space Oddity	1969
James Taylor	Carolina on my mind	1969
Plastic Ono Band	Atomic rooster	1969
Elton John	Your song	1970
Free	All right now	1970
George Harrison	My sweet Lord	1970
Lindersfarne	Lady Eleanor	1970
T Rex	Ride a white swan	1970
T Rex	Hot Love	1970
T. Rex	Get it on	1971
Atomic rooster	The Devil's answer	1971
Harry Nillson	Without you	1971
David Bowie	Oh You Pretty Things	1971
John Kongas	Tokoloshie man	1971

Lindisfarne	Fog on the Tyne	1971
Ringo Starr	It don't come easy	1971
T. Rex	Jeepster	1971
T. Rex	20th Century boy	1972
America	A horse with no name	1972
Carly Simon	You'r so vain	1972
David Bowie	Changes	1972
David Bowie	Starman	1972
David Bowie	Jean Genie	1972
David Bowie	Ziggy Stardust	1972
Elton John	Crocodile Rock	1972
Elton John	Rocket man	1972
Elton John	Tiny Dancer	1972
Harry Nillson	Coconut	1972
Harry Nillson	Jump into the Fire	1972
Harry Nillson	Spaceman	1972
Lindersfarne	Meet me on the corner	1972
Lou Reed	Walk on the wild side	1972
Lou Reed	Perfect day	1972
Lou Reed	Walk on the wild side	1972
Mott the Hoople	All the young Dudes	1972
Mott the Hoople	One of the Boys	1972
Queen	Now I'm here	1972
Ringo Starr	Back off bugaloo	1972
T Rex	Telegram Sam	1972
T. Rec	Solid Gold easy action	1972
T. Rec	Metal Guru	1972
T. Rex	Children of the revolution	1972
T. Rex	Debora	1972
David Bowie	Drive in Saturday	1973
David Bowie	Life on Mars	1973
David Bowie	Sorrow	1973
Elton John	Saturday nights alright for fighting	1973
Elton John	Daniel	1973
Elton John	Goodbye Yellow brick road	1973
Elton John	Stepping into Christmas	1973
Elton JOhn	Step into Christmas	1973
George Harrison	Give me love	1973
Nazereth	Bad bad boy	1973
Queen	Seven seas of Rhye	1973
T. Rec	the Groover	1973
Ace	How long	1974
David Bowie	Rock and roll suicide	1974
Elton John	Candle in the wind	1974
Queen	Killer Queen	1974
Supertramp	Dreamer	1974
Queen	Bohemian Raphosody	1975
David Bowie	Suffragette City	1976
Elton John	Take me to the pilot	1976
Elton John	Honky Cat	1977

Special thanks to Tim Russell & Geoff Noiz for their help in this creating this time line

THE TEAM THAT CREATED IT ALL

THE ENGINEERS

Barry Sheffield	1967/1970
Malcolm Toft	1968/1970
John Smith	1968/1972
Nick Smith	1969/1971
Tony Platt	1969/1971
John Smith	1969/1972
Ken Scott	1969/1974
Robin Cable	1969/1974
Roy Thomas Baker	1969/1975
Dave Corlet	1970/1971
David Hentschel	1970/1974
Mike Stone	1970/1975
Neil Kernon	1971/1975
Dave Hodge	1971/1975
Ken Thomas	1971/1976
Ted Sharp	1972/1975
Ken Thomas	1972/1976
Dennis Mckay	1972/1978
Peter Kelsey	1972/1979
Jerry Lee Smith	1973/1978
Peter Feilder	1974/1978
Nick Bradford	1975/1978
John Brand	1975/1979
Geof Leach	1976/1977
Neil Ross	1976/1978
Julian Taylor	1976/1979
Steve W Taylor	1976/1980
Steven Short	1976/1981
Paul Jarvis	1977/1978
Peter Kamlish	1977/1979
Reno Ruocco	1977/1979
Colin Green	1977/1981
Mike Donegani	1978/1979
Simon Hilliard	1978/1979
Simon Wilson	1978/1979
Adam Moseley	1978/1981
Paul Frindle	1979/1980
Chris Stone	1979/1980
Craig Milliner	1979/1981

DISC CUTTING/MASTERING ENGINEERS

Norman Austin	1970/1972
Brian Snelling	1972/1973
Bob Hill	1973/1976
John Dent	1970/1978
Ray Staff	1970/1981
Howard (Kipper) Thomas	1971/1974
Tim Young	1971/1976
Steve Angel	1977/1979

MAINTAINANCE ENGINEERS

Ron Good win	1968/1975
Barry Porter	1968/1972
Peter booth	1970/1981
Henri Edwards	1977/1980
Barry Spencer	1974/1980
Berni Spratt	1974/1976
Piers Blastkett	1970/1976

STUDIO MANAGEMENT

Barry Sheffield	1967/1970
Malcolm Toft	1970/1972
Penny Kramer	1968/1975
Ray Richardson	1972/1974
Bob Hill	1772/1974
Peter Booth	1970/1981

OTHER IMPORTANT STAFF

Bernie Smith	1967/1975
Gery Salisbury	1967/1979
Bernie Higgs	1968/1974
Dick Slade	1967/1979
Britt-Marie-Young	1970/1973
Tim Emanuel	1971/1983
Jack Nelson	1972/1975
Peter Dennis	1974/1980
John Anthony	1969/1975
Dave Thomas	1973/1981
Peter Turner	1974/1981
Peter Robey	1975/1979

PHOTOGRAPHY CREDITS

Norman J Sheffield: Page 94 all. Page 95 small middle right, bottom. Page 96 top right, middle left, middle right, lower middle right, bottom. Page 99 top left, small middle left, bottom left. Page 157 bottom left. Page 158 all. Page162 all. Page163 top. Page 164 all. Page 165 all. Page 210 top left, top right. Page 211 middle, bottom left, small bottom right, bottom right.

Nigel Grundy: Page 97 small middle right, bottom right. Page 102 middle right. Page 159 all.

Tony Bramwell: Page 98 all. Page 99 all. Page 103 top.

Mick Rock: Page 206 all. Page 207 all. Page 209 top, small middle.

Ray Stevenson/ Rex Features: Page 100 top, bottom left. Page 101 middle right, bottom right. Page 102bottom left. Page 156 all. Page 157 bottom right.

Rex Features: Page 204 all. Page 205 all. Page 157 top.

Nick Bradford: Page 97 top right. **Araldo Di Crollalanza/ Rex Features:** Page 100 bottom right.

ITV/Rex Features: Page 101 top left. **Brian Moody/ Rex Features:** Page 101 top left.

Associated Newspapers/ Rex Features: Page 102 top. **Tom Hanley:** Page 157 centre left.

Harry Hammond / V & A Museum: Page 95 top left, top right.

CPSIA information can be obtained at www.ICGtesting.com
Printed in the USA
LVOW022042120613

338336LV00001B/1/P